Little Caesar

First published in 1981
The University of Wisconsin Press

Screenplay by Francis Edwards Faragoh. From the novel by
W R Burnett. From the Wisconsin/Warner Bros. Screenplay Series.
Little Caesar. Edited with an introduction by Gerald Peary.

First published in this form 2001
ScreenPress Books
28 Castle Street
Eye
Suffolk
IP23 7AW

For information on forthcoming ScreenPress titles
contact the publishers at:

- the address above
- fax: +44 1 379 870267
- email: mail@screenpress.co.uk

www.screenpress.co.uk

Little Caesar

Screenplay

by

FRANCIS EDWARDS FARAGOH

From the novel

by

W. R. BURNETT

Little Caesar

Foreword

The first law of every being is to preserve itself and
live. You sow hemlock, and expect to see ears of
corn ripen.[1]

—Machiavelli

FIRST SEQUENCE

1. **FADE IN**

   EXT. FILLING STATION   NIGHT   MED. LONG SHOT
   A closed car drives up to a filling station, the proprietor
   of which can be seen inside. A slight figure gets out of
   the car; the driver stays at the wheel with motor running. The light in the station goes out;[2] there are two or
   three shots in the darkness. The slight figure unhur-
   riedly emerges from the station and steps into the front
   seat of the car. The door slams, the motor roars, and the
   car careens out of the service yard into the street on two
   wheels.

   DISSOLVE INTO:

2. **INT. LUNCH WAGON   NIGHT   CLOSE-UP**
   of a clockface with a hand turning back the clock hands
   from 12:05 to 11:45.

3. **MED. SHOT**
   The clock is at the end of the lunch wagon counter. Caesar Bandello, alias Rico, drops silently from the counter
   on which he had been kneeling to tamper with the
   clock. To Joe Massara, his friend, who is seated in foreground at the counter:

RICO (with a nod of his head toward clock):
    How's 'at?

JOE (grinning his appreciation):
    Got to hand it to you, Rico. The old bean's working all the time.

Now a sleepy cook appears from a compartment behind the range, yawns widely, and asks:

COOK:
    What'll it be, gents?

JOE (amiably):
    Spaghetti and coffee for two.[3]

RICO (without directly looking at the cook):
    Forget my coffee. (Silently, drawling, addressing Joe pointedly.) I don' wan' it to keep me awake. It's pretty late.

Joe nods his head significantly, indicating that he has understood Rico's purpose.

JOE (carelessly):
    Oh, can't be so terrible late. (To cook.) Got a watch on you, bo?

COOK (indicates the clock):
    Eleven forty-five.

JOE (also looking there):
    That means quarter to twelve in any language. (Playfully poking Rico in ribs.) Well, how 'bout that java?

RICO (shrugging):
    All right. Seein' as how it ain't midnight yet.

Cook nods, then goes out of picture.

4.   CLOSE-UP
Rico picks up a discarded Chicago newspaper and be-

comes interested in a story. He looks with disgust at a cheap ring which he twists on the little finger of his left hand, then turns to Joe.

5. **CLOSE SHOT**
Rico shows the newspaper story to Joe:

INSERT   HEADLINES OF STORY
> Underworld Pays Respects
> to Diamond Pete Montana

Joe glances swiftly at the story, looks his question at Rico:

JOE:
Well, what's that gotta do with the price of eggs?

RICO (snatching away paper):
A lot. Bit time stuff! (Musing.) "Diamond Pete Montana." He don't have to waste his time on cheap gas stations . . . *He* don't have to waste his time on hick cops . . . He's in the Big Town, doin' things in a big way.

JOE (jerking his thumb at the newspaper):
Is that what you want? A party like that for you, Rico? "Caesar Enrico Bandello Honored by His Friends"?

Rico straightens up and draws a deep breath. His jaw sets grimly as he stares into vacancy. He mutters as though talking to himself:

RICO:
I could do all the things *that* fellow does. More! When I get in a tight spot, I shoot my way out of it. Like tonight . . . sure, shoot first—argue afterwards. If you don't the other feller gets you . . . *This* game ain't for guys that's soft!

The clatter of dishes placed on the counter by the cook arouses him from his reverie. Joe attacks his food with enjoyment. Rico disregards his for the time being, studying the paper.

6.   FULL SHOT
     The cook comes into foreground, sits down in a chair, and leans back; he is asleep almost at once.

     Rico looks up from the paper at the cook. Sure that the man is asleep, Rico slips off the stool and, with lithe swiftness, glides to the end of the counter and resets the clock.

     INSERT   CLOCKFACE WITH HANDS PUT FORWARD 12:15

     Rico goes back to his place.[4]

7.   CLOSE SHOT
     Rico's face is stony as he rejoins Joe, but the latter grins at him with huge appreciation of his cleverness.

     JOE (whispering):
         Great!

     They eat in silence for a while. Then Joe picks up his head.

     JOE (wistfully):
         Yeah, there's money in the Big Town, all right. And the women! Good times . . . somethin' doin' all the time . . . excitin' things. Gee, the clothes I could wear.[5] (Grasping Rico's arm with sudden seriousness; his voice becomes colored by an almost pathetic yearning.) I ain't made for this thing. Dancin' . . . that's what I wanna do.

     Rico frowns. In a voice full of contempt:

     RICO:
         Women . . . Dancin' . . . Where do they get you? (Shakes his head violently.) I don't want no dancin'— I figure on makin' other people dance.[6]

Joe looks at him admiringly, claps him on the shoulder. There is evidently a strong feeling of friendship between them.

JOE:

> You'll get there, Rico. You'll show 'em.

RICO:

> Maybe. (Suddenly sits up straight. With newfound determination.) Yes, I'll show 'em! This was our last stand in this burg, Joe. We're pullin' out!

JOE (with a certain timidity):

> Where we goin'?

RICO (with a vague wave of his hand):

> Oh . . . east . . . That's it, east. Where things break big!

The sound of a distant police siren makes the two men prick up their ears. Sound of police siren gradually grows louder during ensuing action until the car stops outside.

Rico stands up, leaning far over the counter looking for the garbage receptacle. Spotting it, he takes the plates of spaghetti and deftly slides the remainder of the food into the pail. Sitting down, he raps loudly on the counter with his cup. Heavy-eyed with sleep, the cook stumbles to his feet and comes to them.

JOE:

> More coffee, please.

The cook takes the cups and fills them at the urn. He hears the police siren and stands listening. With a shrug he turns to the counter and places the cups before the customers.

COOK:

> Anything else?

JOE:
>   Two apple pies.

The cook shoots the pie onto the counter, then listens to the siren.

8.   WIDER SHOT
The cook comes out from behind the counter and goes to the door. Rico and Joe pay no attention to him or the siren. Siren screams outside and fades away.
    The cook steps aside as two cops come into the wagon. He speaks to the first. The other draws his gun and stands blocking the doorway.

COOK:
>   What's the matter, Charley?

The cop does not take his eyes off Rico and Joe, who swing around on their stools when he speaks.

COP:
>   Two cheap crooks held up a filling station on Eighth Street and shot Dinny Graham. We found their car around the corner.

COOK:
>   Hurt him?

COP:
>   Plenty!

9.   CLOSE SHOT
centering on the first cop, Rico, and Joe. Joe slides off his stool, but the cop abruptly motions for him to stay where he is.

COP:
>   Where you guys from?

JOE:
>   Allendale. We didn't do nothing. Our car is out in front—the little roadster.

Joe does the talking. There is no element of fear in either his or Rico's attitude. In fact, Rico assumes a negligent pose, with one elbow on the counter, and regards the cops with subtle derision while he combs his sleek black hair of which he is inordinately proud. This is a characteristic gesture with him. He keeps the comb in his upper vest pocket; in reaching for it his hand is only an inch away from the butt of an automatic, carried in a shoulder holster.

10. WIDER SHOT   (TOWARD CLOCK)
The cook, nervously afraid of the consequences of a gun battle in his place, turns to the cop. Rico and Joe look at their alibi—perhaps it will work without having to bring up the subject themselves.

COOK:
What time did it happen, Charley?

COP:
Five minutes to twelve.

The cop looks at Rico and Joe.

COP:
How long you guys been here?

COOK:
They been eating in here since 11:45.

The cop glances up at the clock in background. Pulling out his watch he compares the time. The clock is right.

COP:
Pretty lucky for them . . . If you see anybody suspicious, let me know.

The cops leave. The cook closes the door and returns to his seat behind the counter. Joe and Rico start on their pie.

11.   MED. CLOSE SHOT   RICO AND JOE

JOE (between mouthfuls):
>Whew! That was close. You got me kinda jumpy when I seen you reachin' for the . . . (Finishes the sentence by pantomiming Rico's former action of reaching for his armpit.)

RICO (shrugs):
>Maybe I should o' done it, too. (Pats his gun.) That's all I got between me and them—between me and the whole world . . . (Pushes his plate away with the half-finished pie.) Let's go.

Rico rises from his stool. The paper is still before him. Once more he looks at it. Then, with sudden decision, he quickly draws the cheap ring from his finger and throws it into a cuspidor.

INSERT   FLASH OF RING DROPPING INTO CUSPIDOR

JOE:
>What're you doin' that for?

RICO:
>No more phonies for me . . . Big shots don't wear 'em! (On his way to door.) Ready?

Joe tosses some change on the counter as we

FADE OUT

SECOND SEQUENCE

FADE IN

CLUB PALERMO SIGN GOING ON AND OFF

DISSOLVE TO:

12.   INT. SAM VETTORI'S OFFICE   CLUB PALERMO   CLOSE SHOT

This is a CLOSE SHOT of a game of solitaire partly laid out on a table. Two thick, heavy hands can be seen hovering over the table, placing the rest of the cards from a greasy, worn deck. Over the screen we hear (photograph Rico speaking):

RICO'S VOICE:
> . . . and that's all there is to it. I beat it east, like I told you. I wanna run with your mob if you'll let me. What d'you say?

The hand goes on playing. There is silence from the owner. During this, CAMERA PANS UP to the face of Sam Vettori as he sits there still dealing the cards off the dirty deck. Sam's eyes are on the cards before him; he appears to be paying no attention to Rico, whose voice we hear again.

RICO'S VOICE (continuing; with pleading earnestness):
> You won't be sorry for lettin' me in, Mr. Vettori. I'll shoot square with you . . . I'll do anything you say . . . I ain't afraid of nothin'!

Now Sam Vettori speaks. He slowly raises his eyes to the still unseen man before him as he asks:

SAM:
> So you think you're a hard guy, huh?

13. INT. CLUB PALERMO   SAM VETTORI'S OFFICE   WIDER SHOT
Now the CAMERA includes Rico in the SHOT as he stands before Sam's table, looking at the other with a certain determination.[7]

RICO:
> Gimme a chance to show you.

SAM:
> What d'you know about me?

RICO:
> I got told enough. How you run things this end of town. (With a wide wave of his hand which indicates the rest of the room.) 'Bout this here Club Palermo—how it's your front. I heard plenty!

SAM (placing cards):
> Maybe you're good with a rod, too, huh?

RICO:
> Quick with it, that's what I am. And sure.

SAM (pausing for the first time with his cards):
> Well, that don't go around here. That's old stuff.
> This ain't the sticks.

RICO:
> I get you!

Now Sam rises. Stepping closer to Rico he looks into the other's face and says in a hard, uncontradictable voice:

SAM:
> All right! You stick around. But I'm the boss and I
> give orders. And when we split, we split my way.
> And no squawks. Get me?

RICO (a flash of joy lights up his face):
> Sure, Mr. Vettori!

SAM (now indicating the room with his thick thumb):
> Come on, meet the boys . . . They're A-1, every
> one of 'em . . . That's Tony Passa . . . he can drive
> a car better than any mug in town . . .

14. INT. SAM'S OFFICE   MED. SHOT
We see Sam and Rico go toward the open door of the office. Beyond the door, not very far in the background is a gaming table with a bright droplight over it. Seated around the table are several men, some of them in shirt-sleeves, playing cards. Tony Passa, Otero, and Scabby are among them. During the walk to the door, Sam continues with a nod of his head in the direction of the table:

SAM:
> . . . and that's Otero. He's the goods all right.[8] An'
> Scabby—what a smart guy! An' that's Killer Pepi . . .

15.   CLOSE SHOT   DOORWAY

into other room as Sam and Rico come in.

SAM:

> Boys—I want you to meet a new guy who's gonna
> be with us. This is—

Boys look up from the card table, but Sam has forgotten
Rico's name.

RICO:

> Caesar Fredrico Bandello.

SAM (digs him playfully in ribs):
> Little Caesar, eh?[9]

FADE OUT

THIRD SEQUENCE[10]

FADE IN

16.   ON INSERT OF NEWSPAPER HEADLINE

> New Crime Commission Head
> Decrees End of Gangster Rule

Subheading:

> Alvin McClure Promises Drastic
> Measures against Thugs

From this,

DISSOLVE INTO:

17.   INSERT   IMPRESSIONISTIC SHOT OF ROULETTE WHEEL
SPINNING

DISSOLVE INTO:

18.   INT. ARNIE'S GAMBLING HOUSE   FOYER   NIGHT

We DISSOLVE in on the shadow of a hand, falling against
a blank wall. The fist is closed, forefinger pointed. Hold
SHOT for a second, then PAN OVER to Little Arnie, standing with Ritz Colonna. It is Arnie's hand that we see
reflected in the shadow; with arm shot out, forefinger
extended, he is pointing toward the gambling room, as
yet unseen by the audience. Arnie, in a lowered voice,
to Ritz:

ARNIE:

> That's your man. I don't know who he is and I don't want to know. But he's too lucky for *my* house . . .

19. INT. LITTLE ARNIE'S GAMBLING HOUSE   MAIN GAMBLING ROOM (FROM ARNIE'S ANGLE: AS HE AND RITZ SEE IT NOW)
This is the usual gambling den; card and roulette tables, etc. The whirring click of roulette wheels comes to us through the noise of a crap game in background.

20. INT. ARNIE'S GAMBLING HOUSE   FOYER   NIGHT
With a significant glance at Ritz, Arnie says while lowering his voice:

ARNIE:

> Wait till he gets downstairs.

RITZ:

> Okay, Boss! (Bending closer; in a confidential whisper.) Sam Vettori is still waiting for you in your office.

Arnie frowns, clicks his tongue with a measure of irritation.

ARNIE:

> All right. I guess I'll *have* to see him. Wonder what he wants here.

With that, he turns on his heels and walks to door of his office, which is at the other end of the foyer opposite door through which we had seen the gambling room.

21. INT. ARNIE'S GAMBLING HOUSE   FOYER   NIGHT
CLOSE SHOT   ARNIE AT DOOR
Just about to open the door, Arnie turns once more toward Ritz Colonna, who is now out of the picture, and says to him in a low voice:

ARNIE:

Say, Ritz, better stick with me! Let that other guy go—I'll need you in here. That Sam Vettori is a no good guy.

RITZ (with an understanding glance):

You said it, Boss! (Gently pushing Arnie aside.) Better let *me* go first . . . (Opens door. They enter.)

22.   INT. ARNIE'S OFFICE   MEDIUM SHOT

We see Sam Vettori's heavy bulk in an easy chair as Ritz enters, followed by Arnie. Rico (somewhat better dressed than in the First Sequence) is standing in a strategic position between the door and Sam. Now his hand instinctively goes toward his armpit—he is ready! But Sam waves to him as though saying, "Cut that!" Rico lowers his hand.

SAM (without rising; with a measure of amiability):

Lo, Arnie! Surprised to see me in your joint?

ARNIE:

Maybe I won't be, after you tell me what you want here.

Arnie sits down at his desk. Ritz plants himself near him, without sitting down; he is studying Rico from under drawn eyebrows. Rico stares back. Throughout this scene the two men continue to glare at each other sullenly.

SAM (bending forward in his chair):

I'll tell you all right, Arnie. Diamond Pete asked me to come up. He's coming up too.

ARNIE (surprised, but agreeably so):

Pete Montana?

SAM (nods):

That's who!

ARNIE:
> Well, if Pete wants you here, it's gotta be all right with me.

Through the same door where Arnie and Ritz had come in, Diamond Pete Montana now enters with a body-guard of his own, Kid Bean, and another mug. Montana is well dressed in a rather loud fashion and sports plenty of jewelry to live up to his sobriquet, Diamond.

Little Arnie Lorch rises from his seat behind the huge desk, and Sam Vettori also heaves his bulk out of his easy chair as Pete enters. Their manner is distinctly deferential.

Pete greets them with limp handshakes.

MONTANA:
> Hello, Arnie! Hello, Vettori!

ARNIE:
> How are you, Pete—how are you?

SAM:
> Hello, Boss!

Montana opens his coat, loosens his muffler (it is winter and all the characters involved in this scene are wearing heavy overcoats where necessary). Arnie reaches for a box of cigars and offers it to Pete Montana, who accepts one silently. Arnie signally omits offering the box to Sam—but Sam reaches over nevertheless and takes one of the cigars.

SAM (with a touch of sarcasm):
> Thanks, Arnie.

Arnie looks at him noncommittally, remains silent.

MONTANA (with an indulgent gesture, indicating the chairs to Arnie and Sam, who are still standing):
> Sit down, boys. I got somethin' to tell you—a message from the Big Boy . . .

The lifted eyebrows of Sam and Arnie indicate that this is unusual and important. A certain awe is on their faces as they sit down, waiting for Montana's words. Montana perches himself on a corner of the desk.

MONTANA (warming to his speech):
>Now listen, here's the lowdown . . . (He pauses dramatically, while Ernie and Sam draw their chairs nearer in listening attitudes.) The Big Boy says . . .

Rico leaves the other bodyguards standing in a group away from the desk and draws closer to the big shots. Arnie's glance falls on him. Arnie stops Montana with a wave of his hand:

ARNIE:
>Just a minute, Boss! (Turning sharply to Rico.) Say, you! Nobody asked you to be buttin' into this, did they? Screw, mug!

Rico looks at him, flashing back:

RICO:
>You ain't givin' me orders!

ARNIE (jumping up):
>Oh! You're a fresh guy!

He starts to take a punch at Rico. Instinctively Rico's hand shoots to his armpit, but Sam quickly intervenes:

SAM (scared):
>Take it easy, Rico. You wait out there for me!

RICO (shooting Arnie a glance full of hatred):
>That's jake with me, Boss! (Exits.)

Arnie gives Ritz a sign. Ritz follows Rico out. Only Pete Montana's bodyguard remains on the scene near the three principals.

23.   INT. ARNIE'S OFFICE   CLOSE-UP   MONTANA

Montana is speaking with a certain pompousness and a sense of superiority.

MONTANA:

> Now listen, boys. (Bends forward, extending his forefinger as he speaks.) Watch this guy McClure—what's head of the new crime commission. He's puttin' on the screws and no mistake about it . . .

24.   INT. ARNIE'S OFFICE   CLOSE SHOT

Arnie and Sam listen with due solemnity, nodding their heads at each point that Montana emphasizes with his heavy fist on the desk.

MONTANA:

> The Big Boy wants me to tell you to put chains on your gorillas for the next few months, 'cause if any of 'em go too far, it'll be just too bad.

ARNIE (laughs, somewhat incredulous):

> He can fix anythin'. That's why he's the Big Boy.[11]

MONTANA (shaking his head):

> Stop kidding yourself. Nobody can square nothin' with McClure, not even the Big Boy. Li'l jobs—that's different. We can spring guys for them. But shootin's . . .? *No sir!* (Stands up and starts to button his coat; to Sam.) It's guys like that torpedo of yours that cause all the trouble . . . (Jerks his thumb toward door where Rico had exited. Arnie grins, nods appreciatively.)

SAM:

> Who, Rico? He's all right. A li'l too quick on the trigger but that's 'cause he's new.

MONTANA:

> Well, it's us that'll swing with him if he shoots at the wrong time. (Pulls his derby hat down over his

eyes, starts for door. Arnie solicitously opens it for him.)

25. INT. LITTLE ARNIE'S GAMBLING HOUSE   FOYER   MED. CLOSE SHOT
The CAMERA is facing the door of Arnie's office. Ritz Colonna and Rico are standing there, both of their hands in their pockets, cigarettes hanging limp from the corners of their mouths. From under lowered eyelids they are watching each other in silence. Just now the door opens and Montana exits, followed by Arnie, Sam, and Montana's bodyguard.

MONTANA:
Now remember what I told you. (He struts to door, stops in front of Rico. Surveys him with a hard glance.) And you—you take it easy with that cannon.

26. INT. LITTLE ARNIE'S GAMBLING HOUSE   FOYER   CLOSE-UP
Rico looks at the great Pete Montana with adulation, then his expression changes to harshness. His eyes drop from Montana's face. Through the shot we hear:

MONTANA:
You hear me?

27. INT. LITTLE ARNIE'S GAMBLING HOUSE   FOYER
CLOSE-UP PETE MONTANA   (FROM RICO'S ANGLE)
His glance stops at a large horseshoe pin in Montana's cravat, then drops to a large flashy ring (we use this ring later).

RICO (meekly):
Yes, Mr. Montana!

28. INT. LITTLE ARNIE'S GAMBLING HOUSE   FOYER   MED. CLOSE SHOT
With a lordly gesture, Montana takes his leave, his bodyguard following him.

MONTANA:
>   S'long, boys.

OTHERS (ad lib):
>   Good night.

Montana and his bodyguard walk out of the picture. Little Arnie turns to Rico to say with a malicious sidelong glance at Vettori:

ARNIE:
>   Leave your gat home on the pianna next job you pull. Yeah, park it next to your milk bottle!

Rico hardens again. Sam swings around, growling:

SAM:
>   G'wan! Run your own mob, Arnie—I'll take care of mine!

There is no love lost between him and Arnie. The latter starts to make a sharp retort, but Rico steps up to him, smiling evilly:

RICO:
>   Yeah, I'll park it! I don't need no cannon to take care of guys like you, Mr. Lorch. (Turns, follows Sam.)

29.   INT. LITTLE ARNIE'S GAMBLING HOUSE   FOYER   CLOSE-UP
On Little Arnie, who stares blankly after Rico muttering:

ARNIE:
>   He's gonna get up in this world—yes he will! A couple feet higher than he wants to—if the rope don't break . . .[12]

FADE OUT

FOURTH SEQUENCE

FADE IN

30.　　INT. BRONZE PEACOCK　　FULL SHOT　　　　　　　NIGHT

Through a menu heading—The Bronze Peacock—we DISSOLVE INTO:

FULL SHOT of the main room in the Bronze Peacock, a smart North Side nightclub. The room is richly decorated in excellent taste; the guests are mostly in dinner clothes. A good orchestra is playing a dance number. A number of people are dancing. There is general movement of waiters, guests, etc.

31.　　INT. BRONZE PEACOCK　　MED. SHOT　　DANCE FLOOR

TRUCK

On the dance floor. Prominent in foreground are Joe and Olga Stassoff, dancing. As they come into CAMERA we pick them up and follow them in a CLOSE-UP.

Joe is immaculately dressed in tails. Olga wears a stunning evening gown. The girl looks up at the boy with a melting expression in her eyes.

OLGA (softly):

Gee, I thought you weren't coming at all! I kept on looking at that door and saying to myself: "He forgot all about me . . ." (But she smiles at him as though courting his reassuring denial.)

Joe smiles back at her.

JOE:

Not a chance, Baby! Wouldn't I be a sap to miss out on such a swell break—'specially with a dame like you for a partner?

OLGA:

We oughta make a swell team, you and me. That's what I told my agent, too, when he brought you 'round. (Pressing his arm; anxiously.) Do your best, will you, Joe? The manager is eyeing you up. I want him to like you.

JOE:
>   Just watch me! He's gonna get an eyeful.

32.   **INT. BRONZE PEACOCK   CLOSE SHOT**
On DeVoss standing near the dressing room entrance.
DeVoss is a sleek maître d'hôtel, proud of his establish-
ment. He is closely following the movements of the
young couple. DeVoss smiles his approval.

33.   **INT. BRONZE PEACOCK   LONG SHOT   DANCE FLOOR**
Toward Joe and Olga from DeVoss's angle. The music
rises to a crescendo and Joe, taking advantage of a clear
spot on the floor, executes a graceful movement ending
in a spin.

There is orchestra stops. There is desultory hand clapping
for another encore, then the dancers drift toward their
tables.

Joe and Olga head for DeVoss. (This shot allows the
use of doubles if necessary.)

34.   **INT. BRONZE PEACOCK   CLOSE SHOT   DANCE FLOOR**
On DeVoss as Joe and Olga enter to meet him. Olga is
breathing quickly after her exertions. She is holding
Joe's hand and pulls him to DeVoss, questioning eagerly.

OLGA:
>   Well, I got hold of a real hoofer for a partner, didn't
>   I, Mr. DeVoss?

DeVoss runs an appraising eye from Joe's glossy hair to
his immaculate boots. There is no question but what Joe
has it. But he stalls, teasing the girl. Olga is on tenter-
hooks and says pleadingly:

OLGA:
>   He's an elegant dancer. We'd panic 'em, working
>   together.

DeVoss smiles at her.

DeVOSS:

You're not trying to sell him now, Olga? (Laughs; to Joe.) Well, young fellow, a hundred a week ought to buy you. That's more than I usually start them with.

JOE (laughing):

Can't get no limousines with that, but it ought to buy me a bit of gas till I get paid enough to buy a car to it.

Olga looks at the two men, delighted. DeVoss laughs.

OLGA:

Gee, thanks, Mr. DeVoss! You won't be sorry for this.

DeVOSS (chucking Olga under the chin):

Olga, when are you going to give me a chance to do something I *can* be sorry for?

Olga takes Joe's arm and leads him toward the dressing room. DeVoss looks after them, then turns to a captain who enters.

35.　　INT. BRONZE PEACOCK　DRESSING ROOM　FULL SHOT

Joe and Olga come into the girl's dressing room, which they share from now on. It is a cozy place with a dressing table, day bed, a chair or two. Pictures of a few movie stars are on the wall.

Joe is smiling over his success and starts to sit down, but Olga stops him. Her manner undergoes a decided change. She holds him by the lapels of his coat and looks up.

36.　　INT. BRONZE PEACOCK　DRESSING ROOM　CLOSE

SHOT　OLGA

as she studies the boy narrowly.

OLGA:

So it's you and me from now on. Well, I'm glad and

I ain't ashamed to tell you. It's no use kidding . . .
I guess you know by this time how I feel about you.
That's all right with you, isn't it? (Her voice softens,
an anxious note creeps into it.) Or have you got
another girl? A steady, I mean?

37.   INT. BRONZE PEACOCK   DRESSING ROOM   MED. CLOSE
SHOT INCLUDING BOTH
Joe looks at her steadily and laughs provocatively.

JOE:
Hundreds of 'em. Sure! Only . . . (suddenly putting his arms around her) what's the difference?
This is gonna be real, huh? We'll make it . . . mean
something . . .

OLGA (softly):
Yeah, Joey. Let's!

JOE:
'Cause I need somebody . . . somebody like you . . .
awful bad . . . Do you believe me, Olga?

OLGA:
I want to believe you . . .

38.   INT. BRONZE PEACOCK DRESSING ROOM   MED. CLOSE
SHOT
Joe takes the girl in his arms and kisses her. Olga's arms
go around him. In doing this, she touches the gat under
his left arm and draws away. Pointing to the gun, she
asks, frightened:

OLGA:
What's that? What you got there, Joe?

Joe casually takes the big automatic from its holster and
slips it into the dressing table drawer. Olga's eyes go
wide at sight of the gun. She whispers:

OLGA:
What are you doing with that?

Joe stares at her grimly, takes her by both arms, and pulls her face close to his, saying:

JOE:
> Can't you forget you seen it? It won't make no difference . . . not between us, Olga. Don't you worry, Babyface. It's just a little good-luck charm I carry with me . . .

Olga wets her lips and nods. Joe releases her. The girl looks at him with a different expression now—there is a glint of frightened admiration in her eyes, but she speaks stubbornly:

OLGA:
> That your racket?

JOE (uneasy, but with a smile on his face):
> Maybe . . .

OLGA:
> I suppose I got no right to ask you. But now that we got an understanding . . . Joe, couldn't you . . . leave it . . . ? (Shakes her head bravely as though speaking the words to herself.) No, I suppose I *haven't* got the right . . .

JOE:
> What would be the good of you asking, Kiddy? Once in a gang . . . you know the rest . . .

OLGA (with all the confidence of her love):
> I don't want to know. Maybe it can be different this time—if we try . . .

JOE:
> I never seen the guy could get away with it . . .

She places her head against his shoulder. He puts his arm around her.

FADE OUT

FIFTH SEQUENCE

FADE IN

39.   INSERT   ELECTRIC SIGN

CLUB

P

A

L

E

R

M

O

DANCING

DISSOLVE THROUGH THIS SIGN TO:

FULL SHOT OF VETTORI'S OFFICE

(The Club Palermo in Little Italy belongs to Sam Vettori.
An upstairs room is the headquarters of the gang. We
need a corner of the cafe proper, a passageway through
the kitchen to the stairs—the upstairs office with closet
and concealed sliding panel leading to back stairs and
alley.)

Sam Vettori, as usual, is sitting at a table playing a
game of solitaire. Grouped around him are Otero, Killer
Pepi, and Tony Passa. (Tony is boyish; Otero has the
perfect poker face—he is a little Mexican; Killer Pepi is
a huge, hairy, ferocious Sicilian.)

Leaning against another table, which is at some distance from Sam's, is Rico. It is significant that he is
standing alone, keeping apart from the group that has
gathered around Vettori. And during the early part of
scene, while the rest of the gang are intent on Sam's
words, Rico continues to study a sheet of paper, which
is in his hand.

40.   INT. VETTORI'S OFFICE   CLOSER SHOT   GROUP

Sam, placing the cards, continues a conversation apparently begun some time ago.

SAM:
> But we gotta be careful. Little Arnie is interested in this here club and if it gets out who pulled the job . . .

PEPI (interrupting):
> Aw, nobody will be wise to us! They're careless 'cause they never been tapped.

SAM (uneasily):
> Just the same, I don't like this whole business.

TONY (very nervously):
> I don't neither, Sam! Cross my heart I don't. (Looking around with instinctive fear.) I couldn't sleep last night . . . I was that worried . . . I don't wanna take chances—not now, the way they're closin' down on us . . .

41.   INT. VETTORI'S OFFICE   CLOSE-UP   RICO
He looks up from his paper; a sneering expression comes over his face as he turns on Tony:

RICO:
> What's the matter, Tony? Gettin' yellow?

42.   INT. VETTORI'S OFFICE   MED. SHOT INCLUDING RICO IN SHOT
Tony bristles, flashes an anxious glance at Rico—but his eyes droop under the steely scrutiny of the other.

TONY (whining):
> Aw, it ain't that . . . only . . . well, gee whiz, none of us want to hang, do we?

RICO (firmly):
> You'd like to quit, wouldn't you? You'd like to run out on us, wouldn't you? You're yellow, you dirty . . . (Takes a step toward Tony, who retreats, his eyes wide with fear.)

Sam who has been watching this scene from under low-ered eyebrows, now barks at Rico:

SAM:
> Hold on, Rico!

Rico reluctantly stops.

SAM (glowering):
> Where'd you get that yellow stuff? If you're so anx-ious to know who's yellow, I'll tell you. It's Joe Mas-sara, your pal. That's why he didn't show up to-night.

RICO (savagely):
> Joe'll be here. Just 'cause he's late . . .

SAM (waves):
> Yeah, I know all about it. Well, I'll just give him ten minutes more . . . Then we'll see . . . (Pulls out his heavy gold watch and glances at it. Rico steps up to the table, plants himself in front of Sam.)

RICO:
> Listen, Sam. Joe is all right. He's the best front man in the world. He can go into a swell hotel and order a suite—a suite—and it's all right. Without Joe we can't pull this job and you know it.

During this speech, Rico has been emphasizing his re-marks by fluttering the sheet of paper in his hand. Sam, who had been more concerned with his cards than with listening to Rico's speech, now looks up. Narrowing his eyes, he asks Rico:

SAM:
> What's that paper?

43.   INT. VETTORI'S OFFICE   MED. CLOSE SHOT   RICO AND SAM

RICO:
> It's this layout I been figurin' out with Scabby . . .

SAM:
> This here nightclub job?

RICO:
> Yeah.

SAM (amiably):
> Let's see it a minute!

Unsuspecting, Rico hands over the document. Sam, without looking at it, suddenly rips the paper in two and throws it on the floor. Rico's face darkens, his fists clench.

SAM:
> Until I say different, nobody's goin' to plan for this mob but me. Savvy?

Rico stands for a second, glowering. It seems as though he were to spring at Sam the next moment. Then he drops his hands, turns away, and walks out of picture.

44. INT. VETTORI'S OFFICE   MED. SHOT
Sam laughs, looks up at the gangsters around the table as though seeking their support, but the men seem embarrassed, ill at ease. Only Tony forces a weak smile. In background Rico is seen striding to the door, which is heavy and has a shutter in it. We see Rico going out through the door. Sam resumes his cards, saying:

SAM:
> Now get on to this . . . You, Tony, will handle the bus and . . .

45. INT. CLUB PALERMO   STAIRCASE (LEADING FROM MAIN FLOOR TO SAM'S OFFICE)
Rico, having come out of door, is now standing at the head of the staircase, anxiously peering down the steps. For a while he is alone, then Joe comes leaping up the stairs, skipping two at a time. Joe is dressed in a form-

fitting, velvet-collared, blue overcoat, his natty derby
hat at an angle.

JOE:
Hello, Rico.

With a wide grin of greeting he shoots out his hand. But
Rico disregards this, as he says:

RICO:
I told you to be here at eight-thirty.

JOE (obviously not telling the truth):
Well . . . you see . . . I was busy . . . rehearsing
and . . . you know how it is!

RICO (darkly):
Yeah, I know how it is! They've been sayin' it in
there . . . (Jerks his thumb in direction of door.)
Only I didn't believe 'em, see! They're crazy when
they call you—*yellow!* (He says the last word with
significance, looking hard at Joe.)

JOE (nervously; with an abrupt movement of his hand,
as though waving aside the accusation):
Aw, tell 'em to . . .

He doesn't finish the sentence. With sudden anxiety in
his voice, he bends closer to Rico.

JOE:
What's the big rush for, anyway?

46. INT. CLUB PALERMO   STAIRCASE   CLOSE SHOT   RICO
AND JOE

RICO (affecting a careless manner, though with a sharp,
hard expression on his face):
It's a li'l job we need you for. A li'l job at the—
Bronze Peacock. (Again there is sinister emphasis
on the last two words; he is watching Joe's face
closely.)

JOE (his mouth drops open, eyes dilated; he backs up a step):

> What do you men? You kidding me or something? (Feverishly grasping Rico's arm.) But how can I take the chance? They're my friends—everybody knows me.

RICO (coldly):

> That's why! Nobody will suspect *you*. Don't stall, Joe.

JOE (desperately):

> I ain't stallin'! You gotta let me out of it, Rico. You gotta. I don't want to . . . I'm workin' steady . . . can't a guy ever say he's *through*?

RICO (carefully measuring his words):

> You're gonna be in on it and you'll like it. The time is to be sharp midnight on New Year's Eve.

JOE (with almost a shriek):

> I won't . . . I can't. (Instantly cringing as Rico pushes his face closer to him. A cunning note comes into Joe's voice.) I can't . . . don't you see . . . ? I'll . . . gee, I'll be workin' New Year's Eve . . .

RICO (straightens with a curious gleam in his eyes and says with a nod toward the door):

> *This* is the joint where you work! Don't be forgettin' it either . . . (Turns to door, over his shoulder commands.) Come on!

Joe, pale, quaking, follows him.

47. INT. SAM VETTORI'S OFFICE CLOSE SHOT
This is the group again. Sam is still dealing the cards; now he looks up.

SAM:
>   Maybe it ain't so hot, though. Maybe we can't buck
>   Little Arnie.

At this point Rico walks into the picture, with Joe a step
behind him.

RICO:
>   *I* can.

SAM (shrugs):
>   You're too good, that's what. (Now he notices Joe.)
>   You were in a hurry to get here all right. Maybe this
>   kinda work ain't to your liking, huh?

Joe lowers his eyes, bites his lips. Rico hastily answers
for him.

RICO:
>   Joe is all right, Sam. He's in with us.

Again he looks sharply at Joe. Joe feels the challenge of
the eyes, looks up, then turns his eyes away once more
answering in a low voice:

JOE:
>   Yeah, I'm in with you . . .

48.   INT. VETTORI'S OFFICE   CLOSE-UP   SAM
With an energetic movement unusual to him, Sam suddenly shoves the cards off the table. Reaching in his
pocket, he produces a rolled-up map.

SAM:
>   Well, let's see . . . Here's the way I doped out this
>   thing . . . (Slides the map on the table. Lays his
>   thick forefinger on it. Then he looks at Rico.) I—
>   Sam Vettori! Not you, Rico . . . nor nobody else . . .
>   that's clear, ain't it?

49.   INT. VETTORI'S OFFICE   MED. CLOSE SHOT   GROUP
Some of them are bent over the table. Only Rico is

standing, his manner aloof as he looks down on the plan. There is the semblance of a cynical smile on his lips. Joe is also at some distance from the table, nervously lighting a cigarette.

SAM (now poking the plan with his finger):
>Here's where you stand, Otero . . . This is your spot, Killer . . . Rico is over here . . . That's plain, ain't it?

RICO:
>Sure! Only . . . (With a definite sneer now, he pokes a quick finger at the paper.) Who stands here? Yeah, the back door . . . ? Kinda forgot that, didn't you?

From Sam's puzzled face, we can guess that he is caught unaware. He scratches his head, then takes out his fury on Rico.

SAM:
>I'm still bossin' this job, you . . . One more crack outa you . . .

50. INT. VETTORI'S OFFICE   OTERO AND TONY
Otero, grinning widely, pokes Tony in the ribs. With a wink:

OTERO:
>Big smart guy, Rico. Lotta brain, you betcha my life . . .

TONY (with a nervous half-smile):
>Yeah, but I'm scared, Otero, honest to goodness I'm scared . . .

OTERO:
>You craz'. Rico, he come with us . . .

51. INT. VETTORI'S OFFICE   MED. CLOSE SHOT OF THE GROUP
Sam is continuing:

SAM:
> You, Joe, will be in the lobby at five minutes after twelve . . .

52.   INT. VETTORI'S OFFICE   CLOSE-UP OF JOE
as he is listening to Sam, whose words come over the screen:

SAM'S VOICE:
> And give us the high sign if everything's okay.[13]

Joe's face twitches. Instinctively he opens his coat and starts fingering his holster, which is significantly empty just now.

DISSOLVE INTO:

53.   INT. BRONZE PEACOCK   DRESSING ROOM   CLOSE-UP   JOE
His figure of the preceding SHOT DISSOLVES into this one—in exactly the same position. But now Joe is dressed in tails again and his hand, which had been examining the empty holster in the former SHOT, is now slipping a gun into it. The revolver in its place, he draws his coat tight over it.

54.   INT. BRONZE PEACOCK   DRESSING ROOM   MED. SHOT
We now see that Joe is alone—Olga is not in the room. With a last glance in the mirror, and a final adjustment of his tie, Joe crosses to door, opens it, and slips out.

CUT TO:

55.   INT. BRONZE PEACOCK   MAIN ROOM   MED. CLOSE SHOT
Little Arnie is entertaining a party of friends at a prominent table near the dance floor. DeVoss is in the background. The noise has materially increased with the approach of New Year. Decorations, appropriate to the New Year. Signs and transparencies. "Happy New Year" prominently displayed. Little Arnie's friends are a vulgar, boisterous lot. They are drinking champagne. Arnie feels important and is a trifle tight.

56.   INT. BRONZE PEACOCK   MAIN ROOM   CLOSER SHOT
Little Arnie's woman—known as Blondy Belle—wants to propose a toast but no one will listen to her. She nudges Arnie. The gambler shouts authoritatively.

ARNIE:
   Ho! Let's have quiet, gang. Blondy's gonna give a toast!

ANOTHER VOICE:
   Sssh! Blondy's gonna turn a new leaf . . .

A DRUNKEN VOICE:
   Yeah, a loose leaf.

The bunch at the table stop their gabble and turn bleary eyes on the blonde who tries to stand up, thinks better of it, and speaks her piece from her chair.

BLONDY:
   Here's to the guy what invented New Year's! And here's to Little Arnie—may he never be left in the Lorch!

This bon mot is greeted with a shout of laughter. Blondy grins with pride at the reception accorded her wit. Arnie slaps her on the back as he would a man, then pulls out a huge role of bills and gives her fifty.

ARNIE:
   Here—catch!

BLONDY:
   Dollink! May you never die—much!

After this magnanimous gesture he looks around the club. The entrance of a party on the other side of the dance floor catches his eye, and he turns squarely around in his chair to see better.

57.   INT. BRONZE PEACOCK   MAIN ROOM   MED. LONG SHOT
from Arnie's angle on a party of three men and two la-

dies who are sitting down at the table across the dance
floor.

58.   INT. BRONZE PEACOCK   MAIN ROOM   CLOSER SHOT
on same group. They are middle-aged, quietly dressed
with an air of authority and culture. The host is a big,
distinguished-looking man with iron gray hair and firm,
clean-cut jaw. His name is Alvin McClure and he is head
of the crime commission. One of the ladies is his wife.

59.   INT. BRONZE PEACOCK   MAIN ROOM   CLOSE SHOT
on Little Arnie who is talking to DeVoss. Blondy is in
scene, listening.

ARNIE (pointing):
    Holy Moses, lamp McClure . . . the crime commis-
    sion buzzard. Bring 'im over and I'll buy 'im a lem-
    onade!

DeVoss doesn't like the idea at all and tries politely to
dissuade Arnie.

DeVOSS:
    Some other time, Arnie.

BLONDY (nastily butting in):
    Go on, DeVoss, do as you're told or we'll wreck
    your gilded joint. Maybe we ain't good enough to
    associate with those high-hat mugs . . . ?

60.   INT. BRONZE PEACOCK   MAIN ROOM   CLOSE SHOT
centering on DeVoss and McClure. McClure greets the
nightclub proprietor as a friend—DeVoss tries to be in-
gratiating.

McCLURE:
    Good evening, DeVoss. Quite a party.

DeVOSS:
    Thank you, Mr. McClure. Er—er—Mr. Lorch, one

of my financial backers, would like very much to meet you. May I bring him over?

McClure frowns thoughtfully—the name is vaguely familiar.

McCLURE:

Lorch? Lorch? (He straightens with a jerk, demanding coldly.) I didn't understand that persons of his type were connected with this place. (Rising.) I'm sorry, Mr. DeVoss, but you might inform "Mister" Lorch that we're—leaving! I came to this place under a misapprehension, obviously.

The ladies start to gather their wraps, McClure impatiently helping them.

FIRST LADY (obviously his wife):

Alvin, dear, isn't it a bit extreme to get into such a huff . . . ? We're being rather conspicuous . . .

McCLURE (irritably):

Do you expect me to fraternize with crooks?[14]

61.   INT. BRONZE PEACOCK   MAIN ROOM   CLOSE SHOT
on DeVoss, Little Arnie, and Blondy.

BLONDY (a glass poised in her hand, ready to throw it at DeVoss):

Well, where is the guardian angel?

DeVOSS (agitated):

Say, Arnie, I certainly put my foot in it. McClure is leaving!

ARNIE:

Yeah? Well, let 'im go and take a flying jump at the moon!

INSERT   COMPOSITE SHOT OF WHISTLE BLOWING. THEN ANOTHER AND ANOTHER UNTIL THE SCREEN IS FULL OF THEM. A NEW YEAR IS BORN.

The sound of the whistles makes Blondy forget the quarrel. She lets out a yell and grabs Arnie around the neck, giving him a sloppy kiss.

BLONDY:
> Happy New Year and see how you like it!

DeVoss ducks in the excitement.

62. INT. BRONZE PEACOCK   MAIN ROOM   FULL SHOT
of the room. The air is filled with confetti and serpentine. The noise is terrific, practically drowning out the whistles from outside.
INSERT   CLOCK, HANDS POINTING TO 11:55

63. INT. BRONZE PEACOCK   FOYER   FULL SHOT
Joe is standing at the top of the steps leading to the main room. He draws the heavy curtains, partially shutting out the racket from inside. Turning, he glances coolly around. The only people here are employees—two check girls, a waiter, a cashier, and a cigar clerk. Joe starts for the cigar counter.

64. INT. BRONZE PEACOCK   FOYER   CLOSE SHOT ON CHECK GIRLS
One of the check girls watches Joe with longing eyes and remarks to her coworker:

CHECK GIRL:
> Gosh! That Joe Massara is a hot-looking guy.

The other nods her agreement.

SECOND CHECK GIRL (with eyes rolled skyward):
> Mmm! Yum—yum!

65. INT. BRONZE PEACOCK   FOYER   MED. CLOSE SHOT
CIGAR COUNTER
Joe stands beside the waiter, who is getting cigars for a

party inside. The clerk looks at Joe while the waiter picks up the cigars.

JOE:
   A package of Egyptian Ovals. Make 'em tobacco!

He flips a dollar bill on the counter. The waiter looks up at the spendthrift—these cigarettes are expensive. The clerk sticks his head in the case, fishing for the cigarettes. Joe and the waiter have their backs to the door.

66.   INT. BRONZE PEACOCK   FOYER   TRUCK SHOT ON MAIN DOOR
With Rico slightly in the lead, the three gunmen come through the front door. Their overcoat collars are turned up, their mufflers shroud the lower halves of their faces, and hats are pulled down so only the eyes show. Rico has his automatic in his hand. Otero prominently displays the evil-looking shotgun. Tony carries a gun and some canvas sacks. We TRUCK BACK as they come into the room and separate fanwise. Rico makes for the office door. Tony the cashier and Otero stay near the entrance.

67.   INT. BRONZE PEACOCK   FOYER   CLOSE SHOT
Joe wheels around, throws his hands into the air as if on a signal, and yells:

JOE:
   It's a holdup!

The waiter turns and nearly collapses, his tray falling with a clatter. The clerk staggers back against the wall. In background we see the hands of the check girls pop into the air.

RICO (out of scene):
   A mind reader, ain't you? Well, keep 'em steady!

NOTE: We see nothing of the gunmen with the victims. They are always just out of scene except perhaps for the muzzle of a gun, a hand, or their shadows. We must handle this very carefully to avoid censorship.

68.   INT. BRONZE PEACOCK   FOYER   CLOSE-UP   PAN SHOT
on the cashier, an elderly, frightened man. His hands are above his head; he gasps like a fish. Tony's voice, trying to be tough, is heard out of scene:

TONY:
    Fork over, Pop, fork over.

The cashier lowers his hands and we PAN DOWN to see him commence dumping money into a canvas sack held by Tony. Only the latter's hands are in scene.

69.   INT. BRONZE PEACOCK   FOYER   CLOSE SHOT
DeVoss's assistant, a Czech with a swarthy complexion, appears in the door of the office. A look of incredulous amazement sweeps over his face and his hands leap up. He slumps against the doorjamb. Rico's shadow comes into scene beside the Czech and we hear his voice:

RICO (out of scene):
    Quick, you! I want a look in there.

70.   INT BRONZE PEACOCK   MAIN FLOOR   TRUCK SHOT
A drunk comes in the door and we follow him. He evidently runs smack into Otero and his shotgun. A lugubrious expression comes into his face; he bows and takes off his silk hat. Then his hands go into the air, and he sidles along to back up against the wall, trying hard to keep his balance.

DRUNK (while putting up hands; with a beatific expression):
    Very—happy—New—Year . . . !

71. **INT. BRONZE PEACOCK   FOYER   CLOSE SHOT**
on Joe and the waiter. Joe is quite brave, even to the
point of kidding. He speaks loudly:

JOE:
>   Wow—a nice little celebration we're having! Fine
>   little celebration . . .

He smiles at the waiter, who looks hastily away with
agonized eyes as if to say to Otero: "I can't help what
that bird's saying."

72. **INT. BRONZE PEACOCK   FOYER   CLOSE SHOT**
on Otero near the door as Tony backs into scene. The
boy has the money sacks under one arm. The other
hand swings a gun unsteadily around the arc of the
room. Otero is a statue; only his quick piercing eyes
move. Tony is gradually losing his nerve.

73. **INT. BRONZE PEACOCK   FOYER   CLOSE SHOT**
Rico backs out of the office door, stuffing a wad of bills
in his overcoat pocket; his pockets bulge. He snaps the
door shut, then whips around and runs into scene.

74. **INT. BRONZE PEACOCK   FOYER   MED. SHOT**
The McClure party come through the curtains from the
main room and stops, petrified. We hear Rico's intimi-
dating voice:

RICO (out of scene):
>   Stand right there! All of you!

Two of the men and both women put up their hands;
McClure hesitates. Suddenly one of the ladies faints
and falls, hitting her head with an audible thump, and
slips down the steps. This is too much for McClure,
who gives a bellow of rage and reaches for a gun.

McCLURE:
>   You dirty, low-down . . .

A gun roars out of scene. McClure takes a couple of steps, a dazed expression on his face, and pitches forward, arms outflung.[15]

75. INT. BRONZE PEACOCK   MAIN DOOR   CLOSE SHOT
Tony is gone. Otero is holding the door open for Rico, who is slowly backing to him, his gun raised, a feral expression on his face. There is no doubt as to who fired the shot. Rico whisks through the door. They vanish.

76. INT. BRONZE PEACOCK   FULL SHOT   REVERSE ANGLE
A woman screams. Everyone rushes for McClure. A crowd forms around him. Joe beats it for the back of the building. Confusion!

77. EXT. BRONZE PEACOCK   NIGHT   CLOSE SHOT
on Tony, who has already started the car. Tears are streaming down his face. He is completely unnerved. Otero is on the running board, holding the door open for Rico, who barges into scene.[16] Tony cannot get the gears meshed. Rico slaps him hard across the face.

RICO:
   What's the matter, losing your nerve?

The boy shivers—a single sob escapes him—but the blow acts like a dash of cold water. He throws the gears into second and the car leaps away.

78. INT. BRONZE PEACOCK   DRESSING ROOM   MED. SHOT
Olga is in her dressing room when Joe staggers through the door. Joe's face is chalk-pale, his hair disarrayed.

OLGA:
   What's the matter? Joe . . . what happened?

Joe supports himself with one hand on dressing table. He is scared through and through.

JOE:

It's all right . . . nothing . . . (Trying to compose himself, forcing a certain calmness which doesn't quite come off.) The joint's been held up . . . They . . . they shot McClure!

OLGA (with frantic fear in her voice):
JOE!

JOE (with a faint, painful smile):
Well . . . now you know . . . (He drops into a chair.)

Olga, drawing back, stares at him in horror.

OLGA (quaking):
It was you . . .

Joe's face distorts under the direct accusation. He jumps as if to rush at her, as if to force her to be quiet.

JOE:

NO . . . that's a lie . . . I . . .

OLGA (her voice harsher now):
You shot McClure!

JOE (his face twitching with fear):
I didn't . . . I swear I didn't. It wasn't me that shot him—it was . . .

But before he can complete the sentence, he catches himself, shuts his eyes, with lips compressed as though to choke back the truth. Then his hands drop inertly to his sides and he mutters:

JOE:

I don't know who . . . (Picking up his head with a certain bravado.) But it's our hips for this job, all right![17]

With that, he gets to the drawer, pulls it open, hastily drops revolver into it, again shutting drawer. But he hasn't the energy to leave the dressing table this time. He just stands there staring at his own image in the mirror.

79.   INT. BRONZE PEACOCK   DRESSING ROOM   CLOSE SHOT
The CAMERA faces the mirror at such an angle that Joe's body is excluded from the SHOT—only his face is visible, as reflected by the mirror. His eyes stare ahead of him, full of hopelessness and misery. After a while Olga comes up behind him, places her arm around his neck. We now see her face also in the mirror, cheek pressed close to Joe's.

OLGA:
     Maybe everything will be all right Joey . . . Maybe he wasn't hurt badly! But you're through with that bunch! You don't belong, Joe . . . you're not that kind. You'll never go near them again.

JOE (sadly shaking his head):
     You can't go back on the gang!

                                                        FADE

SIXTH SEQUENCE

80.   INT. PALERMO OFFICE   MED. SHOT   FADE IN
In foreground stands Vettori, mopping his face with his bandana and looking at Rico, who is emptying his pockets of money. It is quite a pile; he adds the contents of the canvas sacks to it.
     In background Otero locks the riot gun in the closet—which holds a regular arsenal—then takes off his overcoat, unconcernedly walks to the table, and sits down.

81.   INT. PALMERO OFFICE   CLOSE SHOT
Vettori senses something wrong. There is nothing jubilant in the attitude of these two men. They should be gay after a successful job.

SAM (sweating with excitement):
> Well? Well? Everything go off all right? Tell us, for the love of . . .

RICO (without looking up from counting the money):
> Sure all right! I had to take care of a guy.

Vettori falls into a chair with a thump as though his legs had suddenly lost their strength. His eyes bulge; his face grows purple with rage.

SAM:
> A guy? Who—who—was it?

RICO:
> McClure!

82. INT. PALMERO OFFICE   CLOSE-UP   VETTORI
Sam appears to be having an apoplectic seizure. Inarticulate, he bangs on the table with both hands. Finally he manages to gasp with hoarse rage:

SAM:
> What did I tell you, Rico? Didn't I say to make it clean? Didn't I say no gunwork? You . . . you . . . Amore de dio . . . (Chokes with rage.)[18]

83. INT. PALMERO OFFICE   CLOSE SHOT
White with anger, Rico replies:

RICO:
> You think I'm gonna let a guy pull a gat on *me*? He tried to get me! See? That's the way you gotta play this game.

Vettori makes an elaborate, tragic gesture, rocking in his chair as if in pain.

SAM (wringing his hands):
> The head of the crime commission! The Big Boy can't do us no good—not this trip. They'll get us dead sure now . . . What am I gonna do?

84.   INT. PALMERO OFFICE   MED. SHOT
Rico continues automatically to count the money. Over his shoulder, without looking up:

RICO:
> Maybe you better go and give yourself up. You're slippin', Sam.

SAM (still too frantic to react to the insult; he is suddenly reminded of something and asks, his voice trembling):
> And Tony? What'd you do with Tony? Where is he?

OTERO (answering him):
> Gettin' rid of the car—Tony nervous . . . bigga baby, Tony . . .[19]

> CUT TO:

85.   EXT. ALLEY   FULL SHOT
This is a dark alley, only faintly illumined by a solitary streetlamp. Tony's car drives up and into the scene, veering dangerously. All at once something seems to go wrong with it; it swerves to the curb and comes to a dead halt as the engine dies.

86.   INT. CAR   CLOSE SHOT   TONY AT WHEEL
His face twitching with terror, Tony is seen fumbling with the gearshift. But his hands shake so that he is unable to mesh the gears. Again and again he tries. Now he is sobbing aloud—his whole body is shaken—then abandoning his task in panic, he quickly yanks the door open and starts running down the street.

87.   EXT. ALLEY   TRUCK SHOT
THE CAMERA TRUCKS with Tony as he runs, flattened against the walls of the building, his knees giving way under him, his loud sobbing increasing as he staggers along.

> CUT BACK TO:

88.   INT. PALMERO OFFICE   MED. SHOT
Rico is still at the table, automatically counting the
money. Grouped around the table are Sam, Scabby,
Otero, and one or two unnamed gangsters. Sam, his
head buried in his hands, is keening, his mumbled
words not distinguishable. Now, from outside, the
sound of footsteps—someone is running up the stairs.
All present glance toward the door.

89.   INT. PALMERO OFFICE   MED. PAN SHOT
past the group at the table to the door where Bat Carillo
is standing. He closes the door. The men tense.

BAT:
Flaherty and two other dicks downstairs, Boss.
They're coming up.

Rico whips off his coat and wraps the money in it.

RICO:
Stay there, Otero! (To Sam.) They won't know
nothing unless they picked Tony up—give 'em the
salve. I'll be right there, listening.

Sam, scared to death, still sits with his head buried in
his palms. Rico nudges him viciously.

RICO:
Snap out of it, you!

We PAN to follow him as he runs lightly across the room
and slips into the passage behind the secret panel. All
others remain in their places. Sam hastily starts spreading his cards on the table as usual.

90.   INT. PALMERO OFFICE   MED. SHOT
There is a knock on the door. Vettori nods and Carillo
opens it. Flaherty and two other dicks step in, right
hands in overcoat pockets. Sam waves for Carillo to
leave. The bouncer exits. Flaherty walks into CAMERA,

to Sam. The other dicks stay by the door. Sam dreamily plays solitaire without so much as a glance at the flat-foot.

91. INT. PALMERO OFFICE   CLOSE SHOT
on Sam, Flaherty, and Otero. Flaherty hasn't a thing on this gang and is only fishing for information, but he is tough.

FLAHERTY:
Happy New Year, boys! There's a lonesome touring car down the street. Do you know anything about it?[20]

Sam effectively conceals his inward fears, laughs, and shakes his head. From this question he knows Flaherty is not hot on the trail.

SAM:
I got a good cafe business. I don't know nothing about automobiles what's been left.

FLAHERTY:
You might know if some of the smart young guys who hang around here had anything to do with it, wouldn't you?

Sam shakes his head. Otero then asks a leading question.

OTERO:
Wasn't anybody in it?

FLAHERTY:
Yeah, one guy—but not when we got there. He beat it—we got a good description of him, though!

92. INT. PALMERO OFFICE   MED. CLOSE-UP   RICO
in the passageway. He is sitting cross-legged on the floor with his head against the door, listening to the conversation. A flashlight is trained on the money in

piles on his coat on the floor. In the center of it is his automatic—ready. He keeps on counting. His face is harsh.[21]

93. **INT. PALMERO OFFICE   MED. CLOSE SHOT**
on the group in the office. Vettori speaks convincingly:

SAM:
    I keep telling you—I don't know nothing about it!

Flaherty stares hard at him for a long moment, then his glance flicks around the room. There is nothing suspicious here. He turns to the door, addressing the other dicks:

FLAHERTY:
    Let's get going. As long as Vettori doesn't know anything about it.

The other two detectives step outside. Flaherty pauses in the doorway.

FLAHERTY:
    Oh, say . . . you heard the news, Vettori?

Sam silently looks his question.

FLAHERTY:
    Somebody got Alvin McClure over at the Bronze Peacock.

SAM:
    McClure! That's terrible. Some guys are sure. careless with the lead. What a tough break for Arnie!

94. **INT. PALMERO OFFICE   MED. CLOSE-UP**

FLAHERTY (grimly):
    It's going to be a tough break for a lot of birds! Well, so long . . . I forgot to wish you fellows a Merry Christmas!

He closes the door.

95.   INT. PALMERO OFFICE   MED. FULL SHOT
Sam walks over, shoots the bolt on the door, and peeps
through the little lookout window. Rico comes out of his
hiding place and spreads his coat and the money on the
table. Sam joins him. Both men show the effects of the
strain. Otero is unmoved; Scabby and the others come
nearer.

96.   INT. PALMERO OFFICE   CLOSE SHOT
Sam drops into a chair, nerves frayed.

SAM:
It's Tony . . . I can't get 'im . . . The kid's a great
driver . . . must o' lost his nerve . . . (Sighs heavily. Shakes his head. Then, wearily.) Well, let's see
the color of that money . . . (Puts out his hand. But
Rico, standing at the other end of the table, suddenly puts a guarding arm over the money, which
is lying on the table in stacks.)

RICO:
Not so fast, Sam. I got my own ideas of a split this
trip! And you can take it my way or leave it. We
ain't beggin' you!

Sam, abandoning his customary lassitude, now jumps
up.

SAM:
Yeah? Well, I bossed this job and I get my split the
regular way or else . . .

RICO:
How'd you boss this job? By sittin' here in your office drinkin' wine?[22] Well, that don't go no more.
Not with me, it don't. We're done. I been takin' orders too long from you!

SAM (an ugly, menacing look on his face):
And you'll keep on takin' orders, too—or you'll get
out so fast that . . .

RICO (interrupting him):
> Maybe it won't be *me* that gets out . . .

SAM:
> Guess the boys got something to say about that!

97. INT. PALMERO OFFICE   MED. CLOSE SHOT INCLUDING
WHOLE GROUP
as Sam and Rico are standing, they occupy places on
the opposite sides of the table. Sam, as he finishes his
last sentence, looks challengingly at the gang. But the
gang, one by one, slowly move over to Rico's side of the
table and silently range themselves behind him. There
is not a word spoken. Rico stands, a triumphant half-
smile lighting up his face. Sam's face drops; he lets out
an involuntary:

SAM:
> Oh! That's it, eh?

RICO:
> That's it, all right. You've got so you can dish it out,
> but you can't take it no more. You're through!

Sam's face hardens. He stares at the gang. For a while
he doesn't seem able to believe the situation.

RICO:
> Well?

SAM (slowly):
> The splits okay with me, Rico!

RICO (turning to gangsters behind him):
> How about you, boys?

Otero, Scabby, and Bat reply simultaneously:

THE GANG:
> It's okay with us, *Boss!*

98.   INT. PALMERO OFFICE   CLOSE SHOT   SAM AND RICO
Rico steps up to Sam and says:

RICO:
No hard feelings, eh, Sam? We gotta stick together.
There's a rope around my neck right now and they
only hang you once. If anybody gets yellow and
squeals—*my gun's gonna speak its piece.*[23]

SAM:
No—no hard feelin's. If this is good with the boys,
it's good with me!

Otero sticks his head into the picture, addresses Rico.

OTERO:
Can I go see my woman now, Boss?

RICO (with an indulgent wave of his hand):
Sure! Now don't spend all your money on her,
Otero. You worked hard for it . . .

An appreciative laugh from the unseen gang rewards
this, as we

FADE OUT

SEVENTH SEQUENCE

FADE IN

99.   INT. MA MAGDALENA'S FRUIT STORE   FULL SHOT   NIGHT
Ma Magdalena is an old, fat, ugly Sicilian hag. She is a
notorious fence and the confidante of half of Little Italy.
For a blind she runs a small basement fruit store, behind
which are her office and living quarters. She is sitting in
the rear of her shallow shop and as we fade in we hear:

NEWSBOY:
Extra! Extra! Crime Commissioner shot!

A newsboy crosses the store to Ma and sells her a paper.
As he goes away, Rico enters and passes the boy who
exits, slamming the door behind him. Ma Magdalena
takes one look at Rico's set face, rises, and motions him

into the back room. She hobbles after, on her stick. The newspaper is still in her hand. (This is all silent; only by a surreptitious motion of his hand does Rico beckon to Ma to follow him.)

100. INT. MA MAGDALENA'S OFFICE   CLOSE SHOT
One wall of the small room Ma Magdalena uses as an office is lined with shelves of canned goods. There is a makeshift desklike affair and litter of odds and ends.

MA (perching on chair at desk, throwing down her newspaper, she looks inquiringly at Rico):
    Well, Rico, business good?

Rico pulls out his split, peels off a few bills which he returns to his pocket, and hands the bulk of the money to the old woman. During this, Rico is smiling.

RICO:
    Can't complain. Here . . . salt this away with the rest.

MA (while deftly counting the money):
    Had a big New Year's Eve, did you?

RICO (with satisfied expression):
    Plenty big.

MA (having finished counting, she looks up):
    Twenty-seven hundred.

RICO (nods):
    That's right. How much have I got now, all told?

MA (looking ceilingward, her face screwed up as she figures, counting on her fingers):
    Lemme see . . . 'Twas thirty-one hundred—then the two grand you gave me a week ago—and now this pile . . . (looks at Rico.) Seven thous' eight hundred.

RICO:
> Good enough. Hang onto it good, Magdalena. Never know when I'm gonna need it. There'll be lots o' fun, startin' tomorrow.

MA (shrugging):
> Good, you know what to do if things get too hot . . .

RICO:
> The hideout all fixed up?

MA:
> Look at it yourself . . .

101. **CLOSE SHOT   HIDEOUT**
Through this shot we hear Ma's voice:

MA:
> Best hideout in the world . . . Nobody find you here . . . !

This is a shot of the tiny cubbyhole hideout, a very narrow room, not much larger than a closet. It contains a cot and chair.

102. **CLOSE SHOT   OFFICE**
Rico nods. It is a swell hideout. Ma swings the shelves back in place and moves to Rico. Tapping him on the shoulder with her stick, she asks:

MA (wheedling):
> Look, Rico, ain't you got a nice little girl who wants a big diamond?

RICO (scornfully):
> Me buy a diamond for a Jane from a fence?

MA:
> You are cold, Rico. Don't care for anything except yourself—your hair and your gun.

Ma shakes her head and makes a clucking noise. This man is not human.

RICO (smiling):
> I might like a diamond for myself—like big shots wear . . .

The old hag's face lights with avarice.

RICO (concludes):
> One o' these days. Maybe soon . . . (Now Rico notices newspaper on Ma's desk; with a nod indicates it.) Here, lemme see that . . .

Ma, with a knowing, crooked smile, hands him the paper. We can see the large display-type headline emblazoned across the front page. Rico takes up the paper, starts reading it with interest.

INSERT Thugs Kill Crime Commissioner in Nightclub Holdup

Rico grunts. We see his hands folding the paper so as to be able to read the story properly.

INSERT A SECOND OF THE NEWSPAPER
> The thug who shot Alvin McClure was described by one eye-witness as a small, unhealthy-looking foreigner.

103. MA MAGDALENA'S OFFICE CLOSE-UP RICO
His face shows annoyance.

RICO:
> Where do they get that unhealthy stuff? I never been sick a day in my life. (Irritated, he crumples the newspaper and throws it on the floor.)

FADE OUT

EIGHTH SEQUENCE

FADE IN

104. TONY'S FLAT   EARLY MORNING   MED. SHOT

This is a combination living and bedroom in one of those wretched tenement houses that are typical Little Italy. The apartment itself perhaps consists of a bedroom and a kitchen in addition to his room, but we do not see the other chambers at this time.

Tony's bed is made up on a pulled-out davenport. As we fade in, he is lying on it, fully dressed. It is early morning. A feeble city sun sends its rays through the cracks of the room.

105. TONY'S FLAT   CLOSE SHOT

Tony, lying on the bed. He is asleep, but a nightmare seems to be torturing him. His face moves convulsively and he tosses about, occasionally throwing his entire body into the air.

Now, suddenly with a shriek, his eyes open, instant terror takes possession of his face, and he jerks himself upright on the bed. Crouched against the wall, he sits there, his eyes darting back and forth as though looking for hidden enemies. Then, satisfied that he is alone, he seems to quiet down a bit; with the back of palm, he wipes away the perspiration that has gathered on his forehead. Then with trembling hands, he searches his pocket for cigarettes. Finding the crumpled package, he pulls out a weed and with unsteady hands lights it. But after a puff or two, he leaps up from the bed.

106. TONY'S FLAT   MED. SHOT

Tony, nervously moving the cigarette between his lips, is walking up and down the tiny room. Now, unable to stand the torture of his thoughts any longer, he jerks the cigarette out of his mouth and throws it on the floor, viciously crushing it under his heel.

TONY (almost shrieking the words):
> Oh, God! I can't stand it . . . I can't . . .

The door now opens quietly and Mrs. Passa, an old Italian woman with a parchmentlike yellowed face, comes in. She is fully dressed for the street.

MRS. PASSA (coming forward, with a look of concern):
> What's matter, Antonio? Why you no sleep?

Tony comes to a halt, stares at his mother. Mrs. Passa continues:

MRS. PASSA:
> You sick, maybe?

TONY:
> Yes . . . no . . . I don't know . . . (Bursting out irritably.) Can't a guy get up when he wants without having to answer a lot of fool questions . . . ?

MRS. PASSA (slowly nodding her head through this speech):
> You stay out late, Tony? You drink lotta wine?

TONY (turning away):
> Oh! Lemme alone . . .

Mrs. Passa looks sadly at the boy as his back is turned. Then she says:

MRS. PASSA:
> Listen, Antonio, I leave spaghetti on stove. Yes? When you feel better, eat some, eh? Do you good.

She starts toward door again. At this Tony wheels around and asks frantically:

TONY:
> Where you going, Ma?

MRS. PASSA (spreading her hands):
> I go to work.

TONY (hanging on desperately):
>It's early yet . . . You don't have to go . . .

MRS. PASSA:
>I got to go see Mrs. Mangia . . . she has new baby.
>Only think! That will be six.

TONY (with a sickly smile):
>*One* is too much . . . a bad egg like me is . . .

MRS. PASSA (a softer look coming into her eyes):
>You ain't a bad egg, Antonio. You are only lazy. You
>go with bad boys . . . (Stepping closer; her tone full
>of reminiscent tenderness.) You was good boy, An-
>tonio . . . You remember when you sing in choir
>with Father McNeil . . . You in white, remember?

Tony's face suddenly becomes rigid. His eyes stare off
into the distance. He whispers:

TONY:
>Father McNeil . . .

MRS. PASSA:
>The church was beautiful . . . you little boy with
>long hair . . . the big candles . . . flowers . . . re-
>member, Antonio?

The verbal picture has a terrific effect on Tony. Inner
sobs shake him. His lips twitch, he grasps his mother's
arm as he says, almost hysterically:

TONY:
>Don't go away, Ma . . . I don't want you to go
>away . . . don't leave me . . .

MRS. PASSA:
>Antonio! (Her hand goes out to caress his hair.) No,
>no . . . I stay . . . I no go to work . . . I . . .

But Tony cannot bear her touch. He shrinks away, his
voice is harsh again as he snaps:

TONY:

Oh, go right ahead, go! I'm all right—sure I'm all right . . . .

Mrs. Passa, repulsed, lets her hand drop. She sighs, then slowly, without a word, she turns and goes to door. At the door she turns back and looks at her son as though expecting his summons again. But Tony is silent, again he is fumbling for a cigarette, which now he sticks into his mouth without lighting. Mrs. Passa goes out.

107.   TONY'S FLAT   CLOSE-UP   TONY
He whispers:

TONY:

Father McNeil . . .

DISSOLVE IN ON:

108.   EXT. STREET NEAR ROMAN CATHOLIC CHURCH   DUSK
SNOWING   LONG SHOT
A deserted stretch of street.[24] For a while no one is seen in the picture. Then a solitary figure slowly walks into it, headed down the street. This is Tony.

109.   EXT. STREET   CLOSE-UP   TONY
His head is still lifted as he stares hard ahead of him, as though seeking encouragement. Now he nods, twice to himself. He has now reached a decision, starts forward.

110.   EXT. STREET   MEDIUM SHOT
Now Otero lurches into the scene. Otero is patently drunk; he is almost reeling as he hails the boy with a jubilant:

OTERO (at the top of his voice):
Hey, Tony!

Tony stops, notices Otero. His figure seems to shrink and he draws his head between his shoulders, looking out of scared eyes at the Mexican. Otero lurches up to him, slapping him on the shoulder with a great show of friendliness.

111.   EXT. STREET   CLOSE SHOT

OTERO:
> Ha! Where you been? I look all over . . . Rico—he say come and get your split.

Tony shakes his head. He is unable to utter words.

OTERO (staring at him):
> What's matter, Tony? You don't want split, huh? You craz'?

TONY (softly):
> I ain't crazy, Otero, but I don't want no split.

OTERO:
> Listen, Tony . . . Rico know you lose your nerve. Be a man, Rico say. That is good. Be a man. You no better be yellow.

The words seem to strike Tony with especial force. He starts biting his lips, wringing his hands in silent agony. Otero laughs. Again he slaps the boy on the shoulder.

OTERO:
> Look at me! I am Ramon Otero, a great brave man. I ain't afraid nobody or nothing. And Rico—he my friend. I love him with a great love. I, Ramon Otero, love Rico with great big love.[25]

During the main part of the speech Tony remains silent. But before the Mexican has finished his oration, Tony turns and starts walking away.

112.   EXT. ROMAN CATHOLIC CHURCH   MEDIUM SHOT
Having come to the end of his harangue, the Mexican notices that Tony has left him. Now he hurries after the other.

OTERO (catching up to Tony):
>   Hey, Tony, where you go, huh?

TONY:
>   To church.[26]

OTERO (alarmed):
>   Church . . . you mean . . . go . . . confess?

Tony nods assent and continues toward the church. Drunk as he is, Otero realizes what the other is doing and is stunned by the discovery.

OTERO (shooting out his hand after Tony as though to stop him):
>   Hey, Tony, you mustn't . . . Tony, please, not talk to the priest . . . (But Tony is rapidly walking away.)

OTERO (crying out in alarm):
>   Tony . . . Tony . . . no tell nothing to nobody . . . Tony, please.

Tony quickens his pace and hurries away from Otero.

DISSOLVE INTO:

113.   INT. PALERMO OFFICE   MED. CLOSE SHOT
Rico, Sam, and Scabby are in the room, also Bat Carillo, when Otero bursts in. The excitement seems to have sobered Otero and he is quite coherent as he rushes up to Rico and tells him the news:

OTERO (gasping with excitement):
>   I found Tony . . . but it's too late. He's craz', craz'. I tell 'im, be a man . . . but he just shake his head and go to the priest . . .

Shocked by this intelligence, the gangsters look at each other. They are all aghast. Only Rico nods knowingly as though he had expected this.

SAM (gasping):
>   The priest?!

RICO:

> Well, I guess that's it. What'd you expect of a guy that's been a choir boy . . . ? We ain't got any time to waste.

SAM:

> It's only the priest! Confession—that's all!

RICO:

> Yeah, I know. I'm as religious as you are any day. But a guy who'll talk to the priest will talk to other people, too. Get yourself a car, Sam, and let's go.[27]

SAM (suddenly putting a palm over his face with an expression of horror; whispering):

> Not me! Take . . . take Scabby . . .

RICO (impatiently):

> Scabby's no good!

SCABBY (a look of relief spreading over his face):

> No, I'm no good!

RICO (now looking hard at Otero):

> Can you drive, Otero?

Otero hesitates a moment, looks at Rico as though he were also about to refuse, then nods:

OTERO:

> Yes . . .

RICO:

> All right, there's no other way out . . . We'll use the black roadster . . . (Quickly dashes for the door, Otero following him.)

> > DISSOLVE INTO:

114. EXT. CHURCH DUSK SNOWING LONG SHOT
It is still dusk. The snow falls faster now. A black roadster, hugging the curb, approaches and slows down near the church.

115.   EXT. CHURCH ROADSTER   MED. CLOSE-UP
        Otero and Rico are peering through the windshield.
        The car is barely crawling. Otero points. Rico's face be-
        comes as grim as death. He lifts the big automatic which
        has been resting on his knee.

116.   EXT. CHURCH   MED. LONG SHOT
        Tony appears on sidewalk and starts walking up church
        steps. Then Rico's voice is heard:

        RICO (out of scene):
            Tony!

        The boy whips around. There is a fusillade of shots.
        Tony falls without a sound. The gears of a car scream;
        the exhaust roars. (We see nothing of the car or Rico
        during this scene.)

                                                    FADE OUT

                        NINTH SEQUENCE
        FADE IN

117.   EXT. STREET   LONG SHOT   DAY
        As we fade in, a typical Italian procession is slowly
        moving down the street. In the van is an Italian band—
        confined to brasses—playing a slow, mournful funeral
        march. Following this, the hearse, richly laden with
        flowers, wreaths, floral blankets, inscribed ribbons, etc.
        Behind the hearse, a number of closed automobiles—
        limousines, of the kind furnished by undertakers for
        such processions.
        NOTE: Horses with plumes, etc. would undoubtedly be
        more picturesque and quite in character for the funeral.
        But, should it be found more desirable to use automo-
        biles, the atmosphere can still be maintained by the em-
        ployment of the latter. This script assumes that motor
        vehicles will be used throughout the scene.[28]

118.   EXT. STREET   MED. SHOT
        The funeral procession from another angle. A few of the

motor cars are included and a section of the hearse. Now the legends on the ribbons are more clearly distinguishable and bear the routine inscriptions: Rest in Peace, Gates Ajar, etc. If desired, individual names can also be featured on the ribbons: Sam Vettori, Ramon Otero, Mother, St. Mary's Young Men's Club, Alumni Association, P.S. 25, etc.

Throughout this, of course, the funeral march goes on.

119.   INT. MRS. PASSA'S AUTOMOBILE   CLOSE SHOT
This is a closed car, driven by a uniformed chauffeur. In the back seat is Mrs. Passa, Tony's mother. Next to her is old Ma Magdalena. Both women are dressed in black. Mrs. Passa is sobbing aloud.

MRS. PASSA (between her sobs):
> Tony . . . Tony . . . Why you go away like this, why you leave me . . . ?

MA (taking hold of her arm, softly):
> Ssh! No cry, Mrs. Passa . . . please . . . you no can help . . .

MRS. PASSA (keening):
> Why I not die? First my husband . . . then the baby . . . now Antonio, he go too! Why I raise them? Why I see them grow? . . Tony, he didn't hurt nobody . . . He was good . . . Why? Why?
>   CUT TO:

120.   INT. A SIMILAR LIMOUSINE   CLOSE SHOT
In this are seated Killer Pepi, Bat Carillo, and Sam.

SAM:
> We're gonna plant the kid right. That'll look good.

BAT:
> See all them flowers . . . ! That hearse is sure decked out pretty . . .

SAM:

> Well, this wasn't no time to be tight with money. Tony deserved a swell send-off. Poor kid!

PEPI:

> But Rico's wreath beat them all. Big like this . . . (Spreads his hands to illustrate.) And all it said on it was "Tony," not even Rico's name.

BAT:

> Yeah, Rico's no piker.

SAM:

> Tony looks like he was asleep . . . don't look a bit changed . . .

BAT:

> Beats me how they do it.

CUT TO:

121. INT. TAXICAB   CLOSE SHOT

The cab is parked on a side street, unnoticed. In the back seat are Joe and Olga. Joe's face is white, drawn. He is nervously puffing at a cigarette, fingering it feverishly from time to time. Olga holds onto his left arm with both her hands.

JOE (suddenly flinging the cigarette out of the window, he starts hammering his knee with a nervous, impotent rage):

> What'd they have to do it for? Why couldn't they let him alone? Who'd he ever harm? Oh, the dirty . . .

OLGA (still holding on to his arm, now drawing closer to him):

> We shouldn't have come, Joey. I begged you not to come. You're getting excited and its all for nothing . . . *You* can't help poor Tony anymore!

JOE:

I had to come. I had to see them taking him away . . . (Now raising his voice to a tragic pitch.) They forced him into that job . . . He was scared. He didn't want to go . . . (With a final bitter outburst.) Like me. Tony was like me. I didn't want to go neither . . . they forced me . . .

OLGA:

That was your last job, Joey. We'll go away . . . I told you we'll go away. We can get bookings all over the country . . .

JOE (his face drawn in fear):

But they'll get me. You watch and see. Once in a gang, always in a gang. They'll get me the way they got Tony . . .

OLGA (sternly):

No! I can save you. I'm *going* to take you away!

JOE (suddenly breaking down):

Yes! Let's try . . . I can never look them in the face again. Not after this . . . I'll do anything . . . (Very eagerly; a cunning quality coming into his voice.) We won't go right away, though, Olga. That would give it away . . . I'll just lie low first . . . keep on dancing at the club . . . and stay away from Rico. Then when the coast is clear, you and me beat it . . .

Olga, her face beaming with happiness, strokes his arm tenderly.

CUT TO:

122.   INT. RICO'S CAR   CLOSE SHOT
Here we discover Rico and Otero seated in the back seat. For a second or two they are silent. Then Otero says:

OTERO:

> Just the same, it's hard on his old lady . . .

RICO:

> Well, it's Tony's own fault. I didn't want to do it, did I?

OTERO:

> No, you had to do it, Boss.

RICO (nodding):

> I had to do it. When you're in this racket you gotta take your chances. Tony was a good kid, but he was weak. There's no room for that kind. It was to be us or him—so it had to be *him!* This is a tough game— you gotta know how to take it and how to give it!

OTERO (suddenly pointing to sidewalk through window):

> Look, Rico, there's Flaherty, the bull!

CUT TO:

123. EXT. STREET MED. CLOSE SHOT
Standing on the sidewalk is Flaherty. He is in plain clothes. With hands stuck in his pockets, he is studying the funeral procession as it goes past him. In background idle spectators, loiterers, passers-by.

124. EXT. STREET MED. SHOT
This is shot from Flaherty's angle: he is with his back to the camera. As Rico's car passes, Flaherty—now showing his face somewhat in profile so as to establish his expression—smiles ironically and waves his hand with mocking, elaborate courtesy.[29]

125. INT. RICO'S LIMOUSINE CLOSE SHOT
Rico, bent to the window, sees Flaherty and perfunctorily waves back, somewhat irritated.

OTERO:

> Things must be gettin' pretty hot, Boss. What's he want?

RICO (shrugs):

> Aw, he's just stallin'. Hasn't got a thing on me . . .[30]

They sit in silence for a while. Now a long piercing scream can be heard from the outside, instantly followed by drawn-out crying. Rico looks out of narrowed eyes; Otero shivers, crosses himself.

OTERO:

> Tony's old lady . . . she sure is taking it hard.

RICO (with a look of disgust on his face):

> That's a woman for you.

Otero's face becomes mild for a moment. Then in an apologetic soft voice, he says:

OTERO:

> Well . . . Tony was her son . . .

Rico raises his eyebrows with an expression equivalent to a shrug, then pulls out his watch and looks at it.

RICO:

> Gee, we're movin' slow.

OTERO:

> We got plenty o' time. That banquet don't start till eight.

RICO (nods; now relaxes and settles back in his seat; then):

> Too bad Tony won't be there . . .

Otero nods.

FADE OUT

TENTH SEQUENCE

FADE IN

126.   INSERT   ELECTRIC SIGN

C L U B

P

A

L

E

R

M

O

DANCING

DISSOLVE THROUGH THIS SIGN TO:

127.   INT. CLUB PALERMO BANQUET ROOM   CLOSE-UP

A man's hand, about to open a program. Just now his thumb is resting on the cover; the owner of the hand seems to be studying it. (The hand is Rico's. It is important at this juncture that he should be wearing a ring either exactly resembling or similar to the ring worn by Pete Montana in Arnie's office in scene 24.)

The program that Rico is studying is a semistiff cardboard affair, with two embossed angels holding an equally embossed shield in midair.[31] Printed on the shield:

TESTIMONIAL BANQUET
FOR
MR. CAESAR ENRICO BANDELLO
GIVEN BY
THE PALERMO BOYS

Dangling from the shield are two entwined ribbons, embossed, and the legend:

"FRIENDSHIP—LOYALTY"

Below the shield, between the ribbons, are two turtle doves, cooing. The whole cover has a rich frosting of golds, silvers, reds, and blues.

Now the hand slowly turns the page, disclosing the advertising section. This is divided into a half- and two quarter-page advertisements. In the upper half we find printed:

> COMPLIMENTS TO A TRUE PAL
> MR. C. BANDELLO
> FROM A TRUE PAL
> MR. SAM VETTORI

In the left quarter:

> TO RICO:
> REMEMBER THE RIVER
> REMEMBER THE BROOK
> REMEMBER THE FRIEND
> WHO ADVERTISED IN THIS BOOK.
> (Signed) BAT CARILLO

In the righthand quarter:

> COMPLIMENTS OF
> JOE SANSONE (K.O.)
> "Lightweight King of Little Italy"
> and
> HIS LADY FRIEND
> MISS ANGELINA VECCHIONI

The hand turns to the next page. This section is divided into three ads, each one taking up one third of the page. The uppermost one says:

> "BE A SPORT—DRESS TO KILL"
> DRESS SUITS FOR HIRE
> Tuxedos used at this banquet
> exclusively rented by us.
> COMPLIMENTS TO MR. BANDELLO AND
> THE PALERMO BOYS
> PARIS ● ROME STYLE OUTFITTERS
> 642 Fairmond Avenue

And in the ad below this:

> "THE HELPING HAND"
> UNCLE'S
> That's all.

The third ad, occupying the bottom space:
"Ma Magdalena"
FRESH FRUITS AND VEGETABLES
TO RICO
A GOOD MAN HARD TO FIND!

Now as the hand turns the page again, CAMERA PANS UP so as to include Rico's face. Rico is dressed in a tuxedo—obviously hired and while not grotesquely ill-fitting the suit is by no means a perfect fit.

RICO:
    It certainly is a swell-lookin' battin' order! That Scabby is a clever guy to get it up so good-lookin' with gold on it an' everythin' . . .

SAM:
    It cost all the boys plenty money.

(Both during this speech and during the inserts, we hear conversation, shouts, laughter from the unseen guests.)

128.   AT TABLE
Now the CAMERA TRUCKS BACK, disclosing the banquet table in all its magnificence.

129.   INT. CLUB PALERMO BANQUET ROOM   TRUCK SHOT
As the CAMERA TRUCKS BACK, we see the various guests seated on both sides of the long table. (If it is possible to photograph this with the camera running on a track above the table, the progress should be down the length of the festive board. Otherwise the best plan may be to arrange a horseshoe table, with guests ranged on one side only, CAMERA FACING THEM. In the latter case, the space enclosed by the horseshoe should be left clear for action.)
    All the members of the gang are present: Rico seated in the place of honor either at the head of the table or at

the center of the horseshoe; on his left the Big Boy, on Rico's right Sam Vettori; then Otero, Scabby, Killer Pepi, Bat Carillo, Kid Bean, Ottavio Vettori, Blackie Avezzano, etc. (Joe Sansone is an ex-lightweight, slender, small, with cauliflower ears; Ottavio Vettori, Sam's cousin, a husky Americanized Italian about twenty-one; Kid Bean is a Sicilian, dark as a Negro. The others, unless already established, the usual gangster type.)

Every other seat is occupied by the ladies of the gang. Cheap, semiprostitute, blondined, overdressed types. There are, however, no women around Rico. Dangling from the chandeliers are red, green, and white streamers. On the wall above Rico's head is an orange and blue square banner, very much like a college varsity affair, inscribed with the simple legend Club Palermo, accompanied by an equally gigantic monogram embodying the two letters.

130.   INT. CLUB PALERMO BANQUET ROOM   GENERAL SHOT
The gang and their ladies are busily eating. In the course of this, there are various rough pranks played: rolls and occasionally salt cellars and spoons and knives thrown around; a handspring on the top of a chair by one of the younger members of the gang; an amorous scene between a lady and her boyfriend, etc. The din is terrific. Ad lib conversation.

131.   INT. CLUB PALERMO BANQUET ROOM   CLOSE SHOT
HEAD OF TABLE
Sam Vettori rises and, banging the table, raps for silence. When comparative quiet prevails, he shouts at the top of his voice:

SAM:
What the Sam Hill! Ain't this a fine way to act at a banquet? What do you think you are—a couple gashouse yaps? Cut the chatter. Scabby's gonna make a speech.

132.   A SECTION OF THE TABLE   MED. CLOSE SHOT

> OTTAVIO (making a noise like a goat):
>> Baa! Baa!
>
> A GIRL (sitting next to him):
>> Gosh! Ain't that cute!
>
> PEPI:
>> Oh, that ain't nothin'. (Putting three fingers in his mouth, he blows a tremendous blast.)
>
> OTTAVIO (screaming):
>> Wow! The cops! Baa! Baa!

CUT BACK TO:

133.   HEAD OF TABLE   CLOSE-UP

Scabby stands up. He is manifestly ill at ease, embarrassed. He fidgets a long time before launching into his speech:

> SCABBY:
>> Well, fellows, you all know what we're here for, so what's the good of me tellin' you all 'bout it? Rico is a great guy an' . . . Well, gee whiz, Rico, I don't know how to talk fancy but— (pulls a platinum and diamond watch out of his pocket, awkwardly dangling it on its chain) this here is for you, see? From the boys!

INSERT   DIAMOND AND PLATINUM WATCH WITH THE INSCRIPTION

> TO OUR STANDARD BEARER AND LEADER
> FROM THE PALERMO BOYS

> A VOICE (coming over the screen):
>> Come on! Everybody clap like . . .

134.   GENERAL SHOT   BANQUET HALL

Bedlam has broken loose. Chairs are overturned, napkins waved, plates crashed against the table. The women scream; the men cheer wildly. Ottavio jumps up on his chair, and, acting like a college cheerleader, gives the signal.

OTTAVIO:
What do you say, boys? Three cheers for Rico!

Led by Ottavio, comes a regular college cheer: "Rico! Rico! Rico!" Catcalls, whistling, applause, etc.[32]

135.   CLOSE SHOT   RICO
His face is beaming with pride as he stands up and waves for silence.

RICO:
All right, if you birds want me to make a speech, here you are! I want to thank you guys for this banquet. It sure is swell. The liquor is good so they tell me, I don't drink it myself, and the food don't leave nothing to be desired. I guess we all had a swell time and it sure is good to see all you guys gathered together.[33] Well, I guess that's about all. Only I wish you guys wouldn't get drunk and raise Cain, as that's the way a lot of birds get bumped off.

Rico sits down. Prolonged applause. Now Scabby runs up behind Rico's back and, bending close to him, says:

SCABBY:
A couple newspaper guys, Boss. They wanta take a flashlight. It's for the Sunday section of the paper.

RICO (indulgently but obviously pleased):
All right, Let 'em come! They'll have to make it snappy . . .[34] (Pulls out his comb and starts combing his hair.)

136.   FULL SHOT
The photographer and the flashlight man take up their positions in the foreground. Farther back, the gangsters

sit up, posing for all they're worth. There is a general fixing of ties, hasty smoothing of hair, etc. The photographer waves, the flashlight goes off, a cloud of smoke through which we hear Ottavio's scream:

OTTAVIO:
> Eeeh! I'm shot!

General laughter.

CUT TO:

137.   INT. CLUB PALERMO   STAIRCASE   CLOSE SHOT
We see Flaherty with another dick, coming up the stairs.

CUT BACK TO:

138.   INT. CLUB PALERMO BANQUET
Rico is sitting in his place. Sam leans toward him.

BIG BOY:
> That was a bad play, Rico, that flashlight. They may pick you up on that.

RICO (shrugs; laughs):
> Aw, what do I care? Don't I want people to see what the boys think of me?

SAM (tapping him on the shoulder; looks around as he says this):
> But say, where's your pal, that dancer guy, Joe Massara?

Rico's face darkens instantly. His expression shows that the same thought must have been troubling him [all] evening.

RICO:
> He didn't come. He hasn't been around for a long time.

SAM (insinuatingly):
> He hasn't quit on you, Rico?

RICO (sullenly):
> Shut up, Sam. You tend to your business and let me tend to mine.[35]

CUT TO:

139. **INT. CLUB PALERMO BANQUET ROOM   CLOSE SHOT**
Flaherty and the other cop come into the room. Flaherty stands at the doorframe, folds his arms on his chest, and looks into the room.

CUT BACK TO:

140. **CLOSE-UP   RICO**
Rico turns to Big Boy.

RICO:
> What does that bull want here? I'll show him where he gets off. (Angrily rises, pushes back his chair, and starts off.)

BIG BOY:
> Careful, Rico!

CUT TO:

141. **INT. CLUB PALERMO   CLOSE SHOT**
Flaherty still at the door. Now in a low voice, he exchanges a few words with the other cop. They both smile. Now Rico stalks into the picture.

RICO (brusquely):
> Well, who invited you here?

Flaherty looks over Rico's new finery with deliberate insolence. Then:

FLAHERTY:
> Getting up in the world, aren't you, Rico?

RICO (feet planted wide apart):
> What's that to you?

FLAHERTY (still pleasantly):
> Gosh, nothing. I'm glad to see you decked out like

this. You see, I got my eye on you, Rico. Don't forget that I'm your friend. I like to see a young fellow
getting up in the world. Well, so long!

RICO:
Fall down the steps, will you?

FLAHERTY (still pleasantly):
Thanks! (Turns to go. Then, as he reaches the door,
he turns back to Rico.) Say, somebody threw a brick
in Meyerblum's window last night . . . You don't
happen to know anything about a platinum and
diamond watch that was stolen, do you? In case
you hear about it, let me know . . .

Rico, taken aback, is really at a loss for an answer. Flaherty turns again, goes through the door. Rico continues
to stare after him.

FADE OUT

ELEVENTH SEQUENCE

FADE IN
INSERT   A NEWSPAPER PICTURE
reproducing the flashlight photograph taken at the banquet in the previous sequence. Caption under the picture:

"Little Caesar" Bandello Given
Testimonial by Followers

Through this:

DISSOLVE INTO:

142.   INT. BRONZE PEACOCK LOBBY   MED CLOSE SHOT
Little Arnie and DeVoss present in the lobby. Little Arnie is comfortably seated in an armchair near the telephone booth, smoking a heavy black cigar. DeVoss is
standing before him, hands in pockets, a worried
expression on his face. In Arnie's hand we see the
newspaper carrying the flashlight photograph. Now he
throws it on the floor, annoyed and disgusted.

ARNIE:

> A banquet, huh? Rico got far . . . too far! So now he's got to stop . . . I'm saying he's got to stop . . .

DeVOSS:

> Oh, Arnie, are you fellows going to start another scrap? What's the use of my paying heavy money to you for protection if there's never any peace?

ARNIE:

> Don't you worry, DeVoss. There'll be peace soon enough. I'm saying Rico's got to stop—so he's gonna stop, see! He's been nosin' in on my territory and that's all wet with me.

143. INT. BRONZE PEACOCK LOBBY   CLOSE SHOT   JOE
Joe is standing on the other side of the telephone booth, which effectively conceals him from Arnie and DeVoss. He is listening to their conversation with rapt attention.
                                        CUT BACK TO:

144. INT. BRONZE PEACOCK LOBBY   CLOSE SHOT
Little Arnie bends forward and says menacingly, emphasizing his remarks with an extended forefinger:

ARNIE:

> I'm sittin' here, see? I'm sittin' here quiet, smokin' a cigar, see? But a coupla my boys ain't sittin' here . . . They're out lookin' for Rico. And they got their gats with 'em, too. Catch on? And once they find 'im, it won't be no banquet Rico gets—it'll be a wake!

DeVOSS (shaking his head):

> Well, Arnie, you know best. I never met Rico.[36] I don't know what he looks like . . . but I do want a little less excitement around here for a change . . .

Arnie rises, laughs:

ARNIE:
> There won't be no excitement, after today . . .

He and DeVoss start walking off.

145.   INT. BRONZE PEACOCK LOBBY   MED. SHOT
We see the two men crossing the lobby, toward DeVoss's office. They disappear into the office. Joe Massara, from behind the telephone booth, is watching them closely. Now, as the door closes behind the two men, Joe rushes into the telephone booth and hastily drops a nickel into the slot. We hear the coin ringing the bell.

It is at this moment that Olga enters the lobby. As she is only a few steps away from the booth, she hears the bell and glances at the telephone booth. When she sees Joe, she comes to a halt.

JOE (in the booth):
> Phelps 2284 . . .

As Olga hears the voice and the number she picks up her head in astonishment. Her face darkens and she hurries toward the booth.

146.   INT. TELEPHONE BOOTH AT BRONZE PEACOCK   CLOSE
SHOT
Joe is clicking the receiver now. Apparently he is having trouble obtaining his connection.

147.   INT. BRONZE PEACOCK   CLOSE-UP   JOE IN TELEPHONE
BOOTH

JOE (quickly, forcefully):
> Otero! This is Joe Massara. I just got a straight tip. Look out for Rico. Little Arnie's after him.

148.   INT. CLUB PALERMO   CASHIER'S DESK   MED. CLOSE SHOT
We see Otero staring stupidly at the hand telephone for an instant. Now he drops it on the floor and turns excitedly to Bat Carillo, who is standing beside him.

OTERO (out of breath):
　　Where's Rico?

BAT:
　　Got me! He ain't showed up yet!

OTERO:
　　Come on, we gotta find him!

They exit on the jump. A waiter comes into the scene and retrieves the telephone.

149.　EXT. CLUB PALERMO　LONG SHOT
A large touring car with closed curtains is driving slowly past the Club Palermo. There is little movement in the street. Behind the car rattles a big white milk wagon.

150.　EXT. CORNER NEWSSTAND　MED. CLOSE SHOT
Rico is at the corner newsstand, picking up about ten copies of the same paper. The young kid who is in charge of the stand looks at him in surprise.

NEWSPAPER VENDOR:
　　Gee, you takin' all them papers, Mr. Rico?

RICO (smiling proudly):
　　Sure—ten! Ain't I got my pitcher in 'em?

151.　EXT. STORE WINDOW　CLOSE SHOT
Rico enters and pauses in the lighted display window to look at his watch. It glistens in the light. He regards it proudly. Replacing it, he buttons his coat and takes two or three steps. Then he sees a touring car coming toward him, becomes suspicious, and stops. Suddenly he darts into the doorway and stands there, reaching for his gun.

152.　EXT. STORE WINDOW　MED. SHOT
The touring car comes closer, slows down. In it are two

women. The car doesn't stop, but slowly continues, hugging the curb. It passes on. Behind it, at some distance, comes a milk wagon.

153.   EXT. STORE WINDOW   CLOSE SHOT
Rico lifts his eyebrows in surprise and relief as he looks after the car. His face is turned after the touring car as he steps out from behind his shelter.

RICO (to himself):
   Well, that's one on me . . .

154.   EXT. STREET NEAR CLUB PALERMO   MILK WAGON   CLOSE SHOT
In the wagon are two Detroit gunmen. Ritz Colonna, Little Arnie's bodyguard, is driving. As he sees Rico he points and yells to the others:

RITZ:
   There he is—in front of that store . . .

He slaps his feet on the accelerator and the motor roars.

155.   EXT. STREET NEAR CLUB PALERMO   MED. LONG SHOT
Knowing, too late, what is coming, Rico wheels around, all the time tugging vainly at his gun. It sticks. The milk wagon drones into high speed. Arnie's men open up. Three streams of fire shoot from the wagon as it sails past. Rico is hit and falls. Above the sound of the shots is the crashing of glass as the machine guns plow into the windows. The thugs are shooting too high in their eagerness. (Might use shot of window being smashed.)

156.   EXT. CLUB PALERMO   MED. LONG SHOT
A regular knot of men boils out of the Club Palermo: Bat, Otero, Pepi, Kid Bean, and others, all with drawn guns. Curious waiters and some of the bolder guests follow them.[37]

157.   **EXT. STORE MED. CLOSE-UP**
Rico struggles to his feet, putting one hand to his shoulder where he has been wounded. A twisted grin appears; he yells mockingly after the vanished assailants.

RICO:
    Fine shots you are!

(The sidewalk is littered with fragments of plate glass from the windows.)

158.   **EXT. STREET LONG SHOT**
From a parallel shooting down on Rico as he is surrounded by his men. A crowd collects from every direction. The core of it progresses slowly toward the Palermo. From the opposite direction Flaherty, the second detective, and a huge policeman push their way to Rico.

159.   **EXT. STREET NEAR PALERMO MED. CLOSE SHOT**
The two detectives and the huge policeman meet Rico and his gang in the crowd. Flaherty grins in a tantalizing fashion. Rico looks at him sourly.

FLAHERTY:
    So, somebody finally put one in you?

RICO:
    Not enough to hurt.

FLAHERTY:
    The old man will be glad to hear it. He takes a lot of interest in you.

RICO:
    Tell him the cops couldn't get me no other way so they hired a couple of gunmen.

The crowd laughs at this sally—Rico is a great man, afraid of nothing. The big policeman is writing a report in his notebook.

FLAHERTY (still grinning):

> If I hadn't been on the force I'd have taken the job cheap.

RICO:

> Listen, Flaherty, did you ever stop to think how you'd look with a lily in your hand?

FLAHERTY:

> No, I never did. I been at this game for twenty-five years and I've got better guys than you hung—and I never got a scratch.

RICO:

> Don't think you're ever gonna take a ride with me, huh?

FLAHERTY:

> When we take a ride together, I'll have the cuffs on you.

RICO:

> No buzzard like you'll ever put no cuffs on Rico. Come on, boys!

160. **LONG SHOT   STREET**
Rico and his mob start moving toward entrance of Palermo.

161. **CLOSE-UP FLAHERTY**
As he stands looking after Rico.

FLAHERTY:

> I'll get that swell-headed mug if it's the last thing I ever do.

CUT TO:

162. **EXT. STREET NEAR CLUB PALERMO   CLOSE SHOT**
INT. MILK WAGON
Ritz Colonna, bent over the wheel, is driving furiously. The two other men are behind him.

RITZ:
>You saps! Wait till Arnie hears of this . . .

FIRST GANGSTER:
>Aw . . . I hit 'im, didn't I?

RITZ:
>You couldn't hit a barn door, you hick!

CUT TO:

163. INT. CLUB PALERMO OFFICE   CLOSE SHOT
on Rico, who has begun to take off his coat and vest.
His arm is beginning to stiffen, and Killer Pepi helps
him.

PEPI:
>Gee, Boss, I'm sorry. I should o' been with you. You
>mustn't never go out alone.[38]

Scabby enters with a basin of water and a doctor's kit.
He cuts away Rico's shirt and commences to wash the
wound. Rico endures this stoically.

164. INT. CLUB PALERMO OFFICE
Otero hurries up to Rico. Rico is standing there, biting
his lips, as though in great pain, while Scabby is deftly
bandaging his shoulder, binding the arm against the
body.

OTERO:
>It was Little Arnie, Rico. Joe Massara got the tip
>and called up. We no could get you in time.

165. INT. CLUB PALERMO OFFICE   CLOSE-UP   RICO
Rico registers surprise as he hears the name.

RICO:
>Oh! Joe, huh? Well, I didn't think he cared enough
>. . . It was white of him, all right. Maybe I'll go to
>see him . . . (Lost in thought.) Yeah, I ought to give
>him a chance to be in on the next job . . .

166.   INT. CLUB PALERMO OFFICE   MED. CLOSE SHOT
Scabby now has finished the bandaging, and with a last
encouraging pat on Rico's shoulder he lets go.

SCABBY:
    I didn't study medicine for nothin', did I? If they
    hadn't got after me and taken away my license
    . . . (Sighs reminiscently.)

Rico, his wound attended to, again becomes the man of
action. He wheels around, facing the gang.

RICO:
    I'm going to see Little Arnie tonight! (Pointing to
    the various characters as he names them.) I want
    Killer Pepi, Otero, Kid Bean, and Bat to go with
    me . . .

On this speech we
                                        DISSOLVE INTO:

167.   INT. LITTLE ARNIE'S GAMBLING HOUSE   CLOSE-UP
of a gun in Killer Pepi's hand shoved hard into the
middle of a man's back.

168.   CLOSE SHOT
Rico and his men are at the steel door which guards
Little Arnie's gambling joint. A fear-paralyzed lookout
shrinks away from the automatic which Killer Pepi
presses against his body.

PEPI (threatening):
    Listen, Handsome. You tell the doorman we're all
    right or you won't be tellin' nobody nothin' no
    more.

The man nods dumbly. Rico and his men crowd into the
corners so as to be out of sight of the doorman when he
looks through the wicket. Otero knocks. The shutter
opens. In it appears the familiar face of the doorman.

LOOKOUT (huskily):
.   These birds are all right.

The door swings open and before the astounded doorman can open his mouth, he is covered by Otero. The
others push in after him.

169.   GAMBLING HOUSE LOBBY   MED. CLOSE SHOT
The doorman has an agonized look. He is sure they are
going to kill him for his part in the attack on Rico. Rico,
whose arm is bound beneath his coat, speaks to him.

RICO:
.   Where's Arnie?

The doorman gasps like a fish out of water but no words
come. His eyes flick toward the private room. Rico's
glance follows his.

RICO:
.   In the office?

With hands stretched above his head, the doorman
bobs his head in an imbecilic fashion. Rico, Otero, Bat,
and Killer Pepi move toward the office. Kid Bean stays
behind, guarding the lookout and doorman, who back
up against the wall. The Kid leans against the steel door
from where he can cover the gambling room.

170.   CLOSE SHOT   DOOR TO ARNIE'S OFFICE
At the office door Rico briefly outlines his plan of cam-
paign.

RICO:
.   Bat, you stay here and don't let nobody in. Pepi, if
.   the door's locked do your stuff. Otero and I will
.   cover you.

Pepi twists the handle of the door; it is locked. Placing
his huge shoulder against it, he throws all of his tremendous bulk into a savage heave. The door springs

open and Pepi falls into the room. With drawn gun Otero leaps after him. Rico follows.

171. **ARNIE'S OFFICE   CLOSE SHOT**
Inside the office three startled men rise halfway out of their chairs: Little Arnie and his hired killers from Detroit.

172. **INT. LITTLE ARNIE'S GAMBLING HOUSE   CLOSE SHOT IN ARNIE'S OFFICE**
Rico and his men are seen surrounding Arnie and his gangsters. Arnie is standing; now Killer Pepi's gun is against his back. Indescribable fright on his face. The two gangsters are half-collapsed in their chairs, watching the muzzles of the guns that guard them. Rico steps close to Arnie, his hat solicitously removed.

RICO (suavely):
   Hello, Arnie! How's business?

The enemy are covered from either side of the room by Otero and Pepi. Rico pulls chair up to the desk and sits down, calmly taking the center of the stage.

173. **INT. LITTLE ARNIE'S GAMBLING HOUSE   CLOSE-UP   ARNIE**
Little Arnie sinks into a chair and sits with his mouth slightly open. As a rule he is imperturbable, but this cyclonic entry is too much for him. His mask slips, revealing a pale, terrified countenance.[39] He blusters:

ARNIE:
   What's the game?

174. **INT. LITTLE ARNIE'S GAMBLING HOUSE   CLOSE SHOT**
including Rico and the Arnie group. Arnie turns to his gorillas.

ARNIE:
   I don't know what's wrong, but it's a private row. You guys beat it!

The Detroit gangsters, only too willing, start to get out of their chairs. They settle back when Rico speaks:

RICO:
Sit still! You guys are invited to this private party.

Although he does not move, one of them speaks:

DETROIT GANGSTER (sneering):
Suppose we don't want to stay, see?

175. INT. LITTLE ARNIE'S GAMBLING HOUSE   MED. SHOT
With his maddening smile, Rico looks from Otero to Pepi, then back to the enemy.

RICO (pleasantly):
I wouldn't stop you for the world, but those boys of mine have itching fingers.

There is a long pause in which the Detroit mugs and Arnie shift uncomfortably in their chairs. Rico breaks the silence.

RICO:
Arnie, you oughta had better sense than to hire a couple of outside yaps! Especially bad shots.

176. INT. LITTLE ARNIE'S GAMBLING HOUSE   CLOSE-UP   RICO
Rico thrusts out his square jaw.

RICO:
You hired these mugs. They missed. Now you're through. If you ain't out of town by tomorrow mornin', you won't never leave it except in a pine box!

Arnie, completely unnerved, actually trembling, doesn't reply.

RICO (trembling):
I'm takin' over this territory . . . from now on, it's mine.

177.   INT. LITTLE ARNIE'S GAMBLING HOUSE MED. CLOSE SHOT

ARNIE (bitterly):
> You're growin', Rico. This is what you been after all
> the time, eh? I saw it in your eyes the first time I
> met you . . . (With unaccustomed bravado.) You're
> a rat, Rico. But if you think you can muscle in on
> me like you did on Sam Vettori, you're off your nut.
> I guess you forgot all about Pete Montana?

This, for an instant, stops Rico. His face assumes a worried expression as his mind weighs the possible consequences of running up against Pete Montana. Next his
face hardens.

RICO:
> And how's Diamond Pete gonna stop me? He may
> be your boss, but he ain't mine.

ARNIE (sneering):
> Sam was too soft. Diamond Peter could scare him.
> But I ain't no Sam! Sam is through . . . now you're
> through, too!

178.   INT. LITTLE ARNIE'S GAMBLING HOUSE   CLOSE-UP   RICO
Rico stands staring impersonally at Arnie and we cut to
an insert to see that he is studying Arnie's fancy stickpin.

INSERT   FLASH OF ARNIE'S STICKPIN

179.   INT. LITTLE ARNIE'S GAMBLING HOUSE   CLOSE-UP
STICKPIN
in detail, as we later use the same one or its duplicate.
Having impressed the design on his mind, Rico's glance
lifts to Arnie's face.

RICO:
> Nice stickpin you got, Arnie! I'll have to make a
> note of it . . . (Shows him his hand.) See my ring?
> Nothin' phony about my jewelry . . .

INSERT   DIAMOND RING ON RICO'S FINGER
This is an exact facsimile of the ring worn by Pete Montana in scene 24.

Arnie, without glancing at the ring, just stares at Rico. Now Rico laughs:

RICO:
Better quit the racket, Arnie. You got so you can dish it out, but you can't take it no more.[40]

180.   INT. LITTLE ARNIE'S GAMBLING HOUSE   TRUCK SHOT
Rico motions to his men, turns, and walks out. Otero follows. Pepi backs out, covering the boss. Arnie does not move. The two Detroit gunmen sit slouched in their chairs, looking at the desk. THE CAMERA TRUCKS BACK through the door ahead of Rico. Killer Pepi starts to chuckle. It rumbles into a roar of laughter.

FADE OUT

TWELFTH SEQUENCE

FADE IN

181.   INSERT   SOCIETY COLUMN NOTICE
Mr. Arnold Lorch, of the North Side, has just left for Detroit where he intends to spend the summer. He was accompanied by two of his Detroit friends, who have been in Chicago for a short stay.

DISSOLVE TO:

182.   PALERMO OFFICE   MED. CLOSE SHOT
The society item is Scabby's work. He is hailed as a hero by Pepi, Sam Vettori, Bat, and Kid Bean. They are grouped around Scabby, who has a paper in his hand.[41] The others roar with laughter and slap Scabby on the back.

DISSOLVE TO:

183.   MA MAGDALENA'S OFFICE   MED. CLOSE SHOT
Repulsive old Ma Magdalena chuckles over the joke at
the desk in her office.

DISSOLVE TO:

184.   PEACOCK DRESSING ROOM   CLOSE SHOT
DeVoss shows the paper to Joe. Both laugh. DeVoss is
tickled to pieces to think that he is rid of Little Arnie.
But Joe makes a vital comment which turns DeVoss into
a thoughtful mood—he is probably dropped from the
frying pan into the fire.

JOE:
   That means you have a new partner—Little Caesar.

DISSOLVE TO:

185.   EXT. CORNER OF BUILDING   CLOSE-UP
Flaherty reads the notice and smiles grimly, then his
eyes narrow.

DISSOLVE TO:

186.   RICO'S ROOM IN LITTLE ITALY   FULL SHOT
This is a dingy room in Little Italy. Rico has not yet
thought of moving into more pretentious quarters.
   Rico is lying on his bed, in a loud bathrobe—he is not
sleeping, merely resting. Otero is seated in a chair,
smoking.

187.   RICO'S ROOM IN LITTLE ITALY   CLOSE SHOT
Otero looks at newspaper in his hand, then speaks admiringly:

OTERO:
   Now you're famous, Rico. Everybody laugh at
   Scabby's story.

188.   RICO'S ROOM IN LITTLE ITALY   CLOSE-UP   RICO
Rico grins as he lies on his bed, then says:

RICO:
> Yeah, Little Arnie took an awful walloping, all right. You see, Otero, 'tain't no use bein' scared of any of these big guys. The bigger they come, the harder they fall. Yeah, I ain't doin' so bad in this business so far . . . (He absentmindedly fingers his scarfpin.)

189. INSERT   CLOSE-UP OF SCARFPIN EXACTLY LIKE THE ONE ARNIE WORE THE NIGHT PREVIOUS
Rico smiles, apparently thinking of his victory.[42] Now, over the SHOT, comes a knock on the door.

190. RICO'S ROOM IN LITTLE ITALY   MED. CLOSE SHOT
Otero leaps across the room, standing at one side of the door, out of range of anyone shooting through the panel. He looks anxiously back to Rico, who should not be disturbed. Rico props himself on his good elbow, gazing at the door. Seeing that the boss is awake, Otero speaks:

OTERO:
> Who's there?

Ritz Colonna's tough voice answers—we are not familiar enough with the voice to recognize it.

RITZ:
> A couple of right guys to see Rico.

RICO:
> Duck, you 'right guys, because I'm going to count three . . .

ANOTHER VOICE (Montana):
> Hold your horses. This is Pete Montana.

Rico recognizes Montana's voice and motions for Otero to unbolt the door. Otero obeys, standing half behind it with his gun ready. Montana and his bodyguard enter.

Otero drags up the only two chairs in the room, placing one at the bedside, the other a little distance away. Montana sits down beside the bed. His bodyguard takes the other chair. Otero squats on the floor, back against the wall behind them.

191. RICO'S ROOM IN LITTLE ITALY   CLOSE SHOT
The brazen assurance and air of authority that so far have characterized Montana seem somewhat lacking. His manner is a bit hollow. He and Rico eye each other steadily. Montana breaks the short silence.

MONTANA:
> I been watching you, Rico. Any guy that can mus-
> cle in on Sam Vettori and Little Arnie is on the up
> and up with me. The Big Boy thinks the same way.
> He sent me to talk things over with you!

Rico's mind works at lightning speed. What is this pre-liminary to? His glance flicks from Montana to Colonna (latter out of scene). It is unusual, to say the least, for a big shot to make any advances. Then he begins to sense the truth. Montana is getting soft. With this knowledge his arrogance grows.

RICO (affably):
> Thanks. I ain't lookin' for no trouble with you,
> Pete.

MONTANA:
> I guess we got the wrong steer, then. Some wise
> guys told us you was going to edge into my terri-
> tory.

Rico yawns before answering calmly.

RICO:
> Them guys don't know what they're talking about.

192. **RICO'S ROOM IN LITTLE ITALY   CLOSE-UP   MONTANA**
Montana's eyes open, then narrow wickedly. He is going to test Rico.

MONTANA:
You know I used to work Little Arnie's territory and by rights it's mine.

193. **RICO'S ROOM IN LITTLE ITALY   CLOSE SHOT**
Rico's reaction is swift. He sits up and swings his feet over the edge of the bed, bringing his face close to Montana. Rico evidently has put the fear of death into all the gang leaders, for Pete draws away slightly and adds hastily:

MONTANA:
But I don't muscle in on no right guy, see? It's yours now, Rico.

RICO:
It's mine and I won't stand for no cutting in.

Montana laughs and answers with the air of a king bestowing largess, trying to keep up his position:

MONTANA:
There won't be no cuttin' in— Maybe we can team up on a couple o' jobs.

This is a tremendous concession for a man of Pete's standing and Rico is amazed. He glances toward Otero.

194. **RICO'S ROOM IN LITTLE ITALY   CLOSE-UP   OTERO**
The little Mexican's eyes are popping. He grins widely. His idol has outfaced the great Montana. (We use Otero's reaction here, as Rico would not display his triumphant feeling to Montana.)

195. **RICO'S ROOM IN LITTLE ITALY   MED. CLOSE-UP   RICO AND MONTANA**
Rico rises. Montana follows suit.

RICO:

> You and me can do business.

Montana offers hand. They pump arms briefly. Rico looks down at the other's manicured fist.

INSERT   CLOSE-UP OF RING ON MONTANA'S LITTLE FINGER
It is a flashy diamond and emerald creation.

Rico now glances at his own, similar ring in satisfaction, then looks up at Montana. The latter withdraws his hand.

MONTANA:

> I guess we'll go. If you need any advice, come to me.

RICO:

> Much obliged. A new guy has a lot to learn.

The ironic tone of his voice causes Pete to look sharply at the little man, but Rico's face is blandly innocent.

196.   RICO'S ROOM IN LITTLE ITALY   MED. SHOT
Otero unbolts the door. Pete leaves. His bodyguard exits after him. Otero shoots the bolt and turns to Rico, who is staring into space, visioning much greater worlds to conquer. The Mexican sums up the situation with two [*sic*] words:

OTERO:

> He's scared of you.

197.   CLOSE-UP   RICO

RICO (laughs aloud):

> Otero, you said a mouthful. He's soft. He's got so he can dish it out, but can't take it no more! It's my turn now! There's no stopping me!

FADE OUT

THIRTEENTH SEQUENCE

TIME LAPSE TITLE

FADE IN

198.   INT. RICO'S ROOM   LITTLE ITALY

OTERO (helping Rico to dress):
> Look, Boss, you're getting up in the world. Ain't none of us ever been asked to eat with the Big Boy at his dump. Nobody ever crashed the gates but Pete Montana—see what I mean? You don't want the Big Boy to think you ain't got no class.

RICO (feeling uncomfortable; the suit is too big for him):
> Yeah—they rig you up better than this in the stir. You're crazy if you think I'm going out looking like this.

OTERO (convincingly):
> You look fine, Boss.

RICO:
> Yeah—all I need is a napkin over my arm.

Otero tips mirror for Rico to get full length view of himself. Rico is won over.

RICO:
> I guess it don't look so bad.

DISSOLVE TO:

199.   INT. LIVING ROOM   BIG BOY'S APARTMENT

Rico hands hat and gloves to butler.[43] He hesitates about shaking hands with Big Boy. Big Boy crosses to meet him. The host looks at Rico's swell outfit and his eyes twinkle.

BIG BOY:
> Rather lit up tonight, aren't you, Rico?

RICO (self-consciously):
> Yeah—I thought I'd better put on my monkey suit.

BIG BOY:
>That's right, Rico, May as well learn now.

The host laughs and motions Rico to a seat. Rico takes long look around the room before sitting down.

RICO:
>Some dump you've got.[44]

BIG BOY:
>Yeah—I sure paid for it. See that picture over there? That set me back fifteen thousand dollars.

RICO (aghast; whistles):
>Them solid gold frames sure cost dough!

The butler wheels in tea wagon with drinks. Rico takes it big.

BIG BOY (patronizingly):
>Will you have a cocktail or a dash of brandy?

RICO (shaking his head):
>Not me. Never touch the stuff. Never!

The butler passes humidor full of cigars. Rico takes one, lights it, and tips back his chair.

BIG BOY:
>I'm gonna talk and you're not going to hear a word I say. See? This is inside dope and if it gets out it'll be just too bad for somebody.

RICO:
>You know me.

BIG BOY:
>All right, get this. If I didn't think a lot of you I wouldn't be asking you to come to eat with me. You're on the square, Rico, and you're a comer. You got the nerve and you're a good, steady, sober fellow . . . Pete Montana is through . . .

RICO (almost leaping out of his chair):
> Yeah? And I thought he was such a big guy!

BIG BOY:
> He has seen his day. If he puts up an argument it'll be just too bad.

RICO:
> I'll say so.

BIG BOY:
> If I said that you're a Pete Montana from now on—that you were to take over his territory and handle it in addition to your own—would you shake on it?

RICO (beside himself):
> Would I? *Would* I!

BIG BOY:
> All right. It's set! I'm doing a lot for you, but when I get you planted I want plenty of service.

RICO:
> You'll sure get it.

BIG BOY (lifting his glass):
> Permit me, then, to drink to the new boss of the North Side.

FADE OUT

FOURTEENTH SEQUENCE

TIME LAPSE TITLE[45]

FADE IN

200.   RICO'S NEW APARTMENT
Rico walking up and down the room like a proud peacock and addressing Otero.

RICO:
> I knew it was coming. I knew he had his eyes on me. Let me tell you—it's not only Pete Montana that's through—but the Big Boy himself.

201.   INT. LIVING ROOM   RICO'S NEW APARTMENT
         CLOSE-UP   RICO
         as he continues:

RICO:
> The Big Boy himself—he ain't what he used to be,
> neither. Pretty soon *he* won't be able to take it and
> then . . . *watch me!*[46]

202.   INT. LIVING ROOM RICO'S NEW APARTMENT   MED. SHOT
         The butler comes in, announcing.

BUTLER:
> Mr. Massara to see you, sir.

RICO:
> Send him in.

Butler exits. Rico hastens to a chair at the fireplace, sits
down, quickly takes out another panatela, unwraps it, and
inserts it in his mouth. All this is done very obviously to impress Joe.

Now Joe enters, stops in the doorway, takes in the
apartment, letting his gaze rest on each object individ-
ually. Rico is watching him from out of the corners of
his eyes.

JOE:
> Gee whiz, Rico . . . what a palace!

Rico, who has pretended not to notice the other's entrance, now looks up.

RICO (with an air of boredom):
> Oh, hello, Joe! Yeah, it's a good joint. What you ex-
> pect—ain't I got twenty grand tied up in it?

JOE (coming nearer):
> Hello, Otero! How do you feel, baby?

OTERO:
> First rate.

RICO:
> Sit down, Joe.

JOE (as he goes to fireplace and takes chair):
> You sure I'm good enough to sit in such a swell chair? (Sits down.)

RICO:
> Cut the comedy, Joe. (Turning to Otero.) Screw, Otero. I gotta talk to Joe private.

OTERO (with an obliging smile):
> Sure. (Crosses to door. While he is doing this, Rico offers the box of cigars to Joe.)

RICO:
> Cigar, Joe?

JOE:
> Thanks!

By this time Otero has gained the door, exits.

203.   INT. LIVING ROOM RICO'S NEW APARTMENT   MED. CLOSE SHOT   RICO AND JOE

RICO (closely studying Joe):
> Well, surprise you to hear from me? I sorta thought it would be nice to have a little talk . . . like old times.

JOE (ill at ease; he tries an air of innocence):
> It certainly is nice to see you . . . especially like this!

RICO (surveying Joe):
> You're lookin' good, too, Joe. Only a little too fat, maybe. Livin' easy, kinda?

JOE (smiling):
> Not *that* easy . . . Dancin' is no cinch.

RICO (with a queer half-smile):
> But you ain't complainin'?

JOE (fearing what is to come; his smile dies away):
  No, I ain't complainin'.

RICO:
  That's good. (Sits back in his chair.) You're right
  about dancin'. Nothin' like relaxation. Yeah,
  dancin' is fine for a—sideline.[47] (Looks at Joe from
  under drawn eyebrows, studying the effect of his
  words upon him.)

JOE:
  What's the difference, Rico? As long as I ain't
  kickin', why should you kick?

RICO (stroking his chin):
  Who's kickin'? Only, should a young guy like you
  be wastin' his time? I kinda took a pride in you, Joe
  . . . brought you into the gang . . . pushed you
  ahead . . . But now you're gettin' to be a sissy.

204. INT. LIVING ROOM RICO'S NEW APARTMENT
      MED. CLOSE-UP   JOE

JOE (uneasily shifting in his chair):
  We gonna start that again? Can't you just forget
  about me?

205. INT. LIVING ROOM RICO'S NEW APARTMENT
      CLOSE-UP   INCLUDING BOTH

RICO (with a certain softness in his voice):
  How can I forget about my pal, Joe? We started off
  together—we gotta keep on goin' along together.
  Who else have I got to give a hang about? (Now he
  jumps up, goes over to Joe.) I need *you*, Joe. Just
  before you came, I was over to see the Big Boy. He
  handed me the whole *North Side*. But it's too big for
  one man to handle alone . . . I need somebody—a
  guy like you—somebody I can trust, somebody to
  work in with me.

Joe shakes his head.

JOE:
    It can't be me, Buddy. I've quit.

Fierce rage takes possession of Rico's face. He grabs Joe by the shoulder:

RICO:
    You didn't quit! Nobody ever quit me. Get that! You're still in my gang. I don't care how many fancy dames you got stickin' on to you. That skirt can go hang. It's *her* that's made a softy outa you.

JOE (a menacing look coming into his face):
    You lay off Olga, Rico!

RICO (furiously):
    I ain't layin' off her. I'm after her. She an' me can't both have you. One of us has gotta lose—an' it ain't gonna be me! There's ways of stoppin' that dame . . . !

As he says the last sentence, he makes his old significant gesture of reaching for his gun.

JOE (terror-stricken as he interprets the movement):
    You're crazy! Leave her out of this . . .

RICO (his face distorted with rage now; he is fairly shrieking):
    It's curtains for her, see? She's through . . . she's out of the way . . . that's what she is!

JOE (drawing back; almost insanely):
    You're lyin'. You wouldn't . . .

RICO:
    I *wouldn't?* I'll show you . . . that dirty, painted-up . . .

JOE (almost shrieking):
> I love her! We're in love! Don't that mean nothin' to you?

RICO:
> Nothin'! Less than nothin'! Love—soft stuff! When she's got you, you ain't safe . . . you know too much. I ain't takin' no chances. You're stayin' here!

JOE:
> I'm not![48]

RICO (gripping his shoulder):
> You move an' it's suicide . . . suicide for *both* o' you!

206.   INT. LIVING ROOM RICO'S NEW APARTMENT   CLOSE-UP
JOE
Joe, almost paralyzed with fear, sinks back against the chair, drops into it. He shuts his eyes and puts a guarding hand up against his face.

JOE (hoarsely):
> No . . . no, no . . .

207.   INT. LIVING ROOM RICO'S NEW APARTMENT   MED CLOSE SHOT
Rico, a look of evil satisfaction on his face, stands over the boy, closely studying him. He is about to say something, as the telephone rings from outside the room. Irritated, Rico glaces toward the door. Then he starts off, with a suspicious glance at Joe. Joe rises—instantly Rico turns and roughly thrusts him back in his chair.

RICO:
> Don't you move or I'll . . .

Joe, limp, remains in his chair. We see Rico exiting through door leading to bedroom.

208.   INT. LIVING ROOM RICO'S NEW APARTMENT   CLOSE-UP
       JOE
       as he sits, trembling in his chair, his face moving convulsively.

       JOE:
            No . . . no . . .

       Over the SHOT, from the other room we hear Rico's voice at the telephone. His words are unintelligible.[49] Joe, once more, now hysterically:

       JOE:
            No . . . Olga . . . no . . .

       Suddenly he jumps up, looks around—indescribable fear on his face—once more looks at the door from behind which we hear Rico's voice, and blindly dashes toward door.

209.   INT. LIVING ROOM RICO'S NEW APARTMENT   FULL SHOT
       Joe dashes to door, through which he had originally come—his movements unsteady—and bursts through it. Hold SHOT after his exit. Rico's words still continue on the telephone.

                                                    FADE OUT

                     FOURTEENTH SEQUENCE[50]

       FADE IN
210.   INT. OLGA'S APARTMENT   LATE AFTERNOON   LIVING
       ROOM   MED. SHOT
       This is a modest enough, very orderly little living room in Olga's apartment. As we fade in, Olga is nervously walking up and down the room. From the impatient little noises she makes with her tongue, from her manner of repeatedly glancing at her wristwatch, from her occasional slapping of her palm against the knuckle of her other hand, we are instantly aware of her impatience and agitation. Now, apparently unable to control herself any longer, she rushes to the telephone.

211.   INT. OLGA'S APARTMENT   LIVING ROOM   CLOSE-UP
OLGA

OLGA (calling into telephone):
Greenhill 0139.

There is a moment's wait, during which she bites her lips, her face again and again assuming a tense, listening expression. Finally there is a voice at the other end.

OLGA (her voice trembling with excitement):
Bronze Peacock? This is Olga Stassoff . . . yes, Olga
. . . Mr. DeVoss? Listen, has Joe been around there?
(Her face drops; the answer is apparently disappointing.) Oh . . . ! I just thought . . . He's been
gone all afternoon . . . Went to see Rico . . .

It is plain that DeVoss is trying to calm her fears, because Olga now answers.

OLGA:
It's just that I'm worried . . . I don't know why
. . . but he was to be here an hour ago and hasn't
come yet . . . I'm afraid . . .

DeVoss again says something. Now Olga essays a little laugh. Passing her hand over her forehead, she says:

OLGA:
Yes, I suppose it's all right . . . It was just a funny
feeling I had . . . Thanks, Mr. DeVoss. Good-bye!
(Limply puts down receiver.)

Now, from outside a bell is heard. Its sound is a distinct shock to Olga, who jumps up in instant terror. She holds her hands to her breast, gasping for breath.[51]

212.   INT. OLGA'S APARTMENT   LIVING ROOM   MED. SHOT
Olga hurries across the room to the door. This door opens directly on the staircase landing, without a hallway—a not uncommon feature of old-fashioned apartment houses. She tears the door open.

213. INT. OLGA'S APARTMENT LIVING ROOM MED. CLOSE SHOT

as Olga is opening the door. Joe bursts in, out of breath, his face pale as a sheet. He tries to speak, but words fail to come from him. He stands in the doorway for a second, his hand on the outside knob, then thrusts himself into the room, closing the door behind him. He leans against it with his two palms against it. He stares at Olga with eyes wide open, clouded by terror.

OLGA:
Joe . . . Joey . . . What is it? What's the matter?

Joe gasps for breath. Then his hand shoots out, the words wheezing out of him:

JOE:
We gotta go . . . Come on . . . Hurry!

OLGA:
But Joe, you're . . .

JOE (frantic with fear):
What are you standing there for? Didn't you hear me? Hurry! Hurry!

OLGA:
Yes, Joey . . . Just let me get my things . . . (Goes up to him, putting her hand on his arm in sudden alarm.) Honey . . . you're going to faint in a minute.

JOE (thrusts her arm away; almost hysterically; shaking his head):
No, I'll be all right . . . Let's get out of here . . . We . . . Rico . . .

His voicing of the name seems to bring back memories of his visit. His face distorts; his eyelids droop. He sinks against the table standing next to the wall.

OLGA (herself blanching at the name):
> What'd he do to you? Oh, I knew it! Didn't I know it?

JOE (desperately struggling to overcome his dizziness; his voice rising and falling away; feverishly):
> He, Rico . . . told me you and I gotta quit . . . That he'll kill you 'less I stick with him . . . I ran away . . . Don't you see we gotta go . . . ? Anywhere! Anyplace . . . out o' town . . . so long as we get away . . .

During his speech, Olga stands before him, slowly shaking her head. Now Joe stares at her.

JOE:
> *No?* You're . . . not . . . coming?

OLGA:
> No! That's not the way!

JOE (grasping her arm):
> Olga, we've got to . . . You don't know that guy . . . You're . . . Olga . . . Please . . .

OLGA:
> No! Sit down, Joey . . . We've got to think . . .

JOE (shrieking):
> I don't want to think. I don't want to sit down. You're . . . you're comin' . . . (He makes as though to grab her arm.)

OLGA (catching his hand and pinning it down against his body; there is a great firmness and determination in her voice):
> Don't you see that would be no use? Where could we go? Where could we run to? There's no place he wouldn't find us. (Staring at Joe fixedly.) Only one thing for us to do. *Flaherty!*

JOE (his jaw drops; he stares at the girl; then):
>You crazy? Do you think that'd save us? *Flaherty!* That's worse than suicide. I can't do it, I won't do it . . . not if both of us have to die a million times . . .

OLGA (firmly):
>*I* can do it! The gang must go. Rico must go. I want my happiness. I want you. We'll never have any peace till Rico is gone . . . I'm *going* to do it!

214. INT. LIVING ROOM
Olga starts toward bedroom where telephone is. Joe guesses her intention and tries to stop her.

JOE:
>Olga . . . stay here . . . don't . . .

But she is quicker than he is and gets into bedroom and slams door shut before he can stop her.

215. CLOSE-UP BEDROOM SIDE OF DOOR
Olga is locking door. On other side of door, we hear Joe pounding.

JOE (yelling):
>Olga . . . open the door . . . don't call Flaherty . . . Olga! Please . . . Rico'll kill us both.

216. INT. BEDROOM CLOSE SHOT OLGA AT PHONE

OLGA:
>Park 1000 . . .

Outside the door, Joe is pounding and yelling.

OLGA:
>Headquarters? I want Sergeant Flaherty!

217. **CLOSE SHOT JOE LIVING ROOM**
As he hears the name, Joe renews his efforts to batter down door.

218. **CLOSE SHOT OLGA BEDROOM**

OLGA:
Sergeant Flaherty? This is Olga Stassoff . . . I've got Joe Massara with me . . . in my apartment, 17 Edgelow Drive . . . He wants to talk to you . . . Hurry . . .

Now she lets the telephone drop and sinks back exhausted.

CUT TO:

219. **INT. DETECTIVE HEADQUARTERS CLOSE-UP FLAHERTY**
He is just replacing the receiver on its hook; he stares into the mouthpiece for a moment, lost in thought. Then a smile comes to his face and he turns to his partner:

FLAHERTY:
Come on, sweetheart!

220. **INT. DETECTIVE HEADQUARTERS MED. CLOSE SHOT**
The other detective, his partner, rises. Yawns.

SECOND DETECTIVE:
Who's giving the cocktail party?

FLAHERTY (with immense satisfaction in his voice):
Joe Massara.

The other detective's eyes open wide in surprise. He whistles softly.

FLAHERTY:
Got the artillery on you?[52] (He examines his own holster.)

CUT TO:

221.   INT. OLGA'S APARTMENT   LIVING ROOM   MED. CLOSE
        SHOT

        JOE:

>   You shouldn't have done it . . . you shouldn't
>   have . . .

        OLGA (who is standing near the table):

>   There was no other way . . . no other right
>   way . . .

        JOE:

>   It's the rope for me.

        OLGA (Firmly):

>   No! Not if you turn state's evidence. We'll make
>   them promise that . . .

                                                    CUT TO:

222.   EXT. OLGA'S APARTMENT HOUSE   VERY LONG SHOT
        Olga's house is one of many in a row of brownstone
        fronts. A machine draws up. As it slows down and be-
        fore it has a chance to stop two men jump out of it and
        dash up the stoop. Only now does the machine come to
        a halt.
            NOTE: The two men running up the steps are Rico and
        Otero. But as it is essential for the audience to believe
        they are Flaherty and his partner, the shot should be
        taken in such a manner as to make the two figures un-
        recognizable.[53]

223.   INT. HALLWAY OLGA'S APARTMENT HOUSE
        Olga's house is a walk-up affair. It is a dark, winding
        staircase, full of obscuring shadows. We see the two
        men rushing up the steps. Again we must not be able
        to tell who they are.

224.   INT. OLGA'S LIVING ROOM   MEDIUM SHOT
        Joe sits up in his chair. He is hearing the footsteps out-
        side.

JOE (teeth chattering with fright):
   It's them . . .

He jumps up and cowers against the wall.

OLGA (also listening):
   Yes. (Starts for door, giving Joe's hand a passing touch.) Stick it out! You can do it!

JOE (catching hold of her hand):
   Wait . . . Olga, I . . .

But it is too late. At this moment the door bursts open, under the battering strength of Otero's shoulder. Instantly he steps through the crack . . . followed by Rico.

OTERO:
   There he is . . . the yellow double-crosser . . . Give it to 'im, Rico!

225. INT. OLGA'S LIVING ROOM   CLOSE SHOT
   Olga reels back, then frantically throws her arms around Joe. She is about to scream, but her terror is so great that the sound freezes on her lips.

226. INT. OLGA'S LIVING ROOM   CLOSE-UP   RICO
   Rico reaches into his pocket, then slowly raises his hand. The muzzle of the gun sticking through the cloth of the pocket is pointed at Joe. Rico's face is twisted into an awful mask of pain.

227. INT. OLGA'S LIVING ROOM   CLOSE-UP   JOE
   He stands against the wall, arms spread out. In the failing light of the afternoon he resembles a figure crucified. He shuts his eyes, waiting for the shot.

228. INT. OLGA'S LIVING ROOM   MED. SHOT
   Olga is about to rush at Rico, who still stands there with his gun poised, watching Joe. Otero, similarly aiming his pocketed gun at her, holds her in check. Joe now

staggers, stumbles; he is on his knees, eyes closed, his arms again shoot out in front of him in a piteous gesture.[54]

JOE (screaming):
    Shoot! Shoot! Get it over with!

Rico draws back—his hand drops—he can not pull the trigger.

RICO (in a gruff voice, to Otero):
    Let's go, Otero . . . *I can't!*

OTERO (shooting Rico a look full of surprise that instantly changes to hatred):
    You're gettin' soft, too!

He wheels around, jerks out his gun, and fires at Joe. Rico hits the little man's arm up just in time and the bullet goes wild. Joe staggers back, holding his wounded shoulder.

CUT TO:

229. EXT. APARTMENT HOUSE   MED. SHOT
Another machine stops. Flaherty and his partner, accompanied by a third dick, jump out of it. At this moment a shot rings out above, followed by Olga's scream. The three detectives halt for an instant, look up toward the window from where the sounds issued, then dash up the steps, disappearing through the door of the house.

CUT BACK TO:

230. INT. APARTMENT HOUSE   MED. SHOT
Rico is just wresting the automatic away from Otero, his look menacing the Mexican.

RICO:
    Gimme that, you . . .

The Mexican seems to be putting up a fight. The two men struggle for the possession of the gun. Rico succeeds in tearing the weapon from the Mexican and they dash to door. But at this moment, from outside, we hear voices.

FLAHERTY'S PARTNER'S VOICE:
    What floor?

Rico stops short, stares at the door, like an animal at bay. Now, from outside, another voice answers the first:

FLAHERTY'S VOICE:
    The third! Come on, boys!

Rico leaps back, wheels around, dashes to window, Otero after him.[55]

231.   INT. OLGA'S LIVING ROOM   CLOSE SHOT AT WINDOW
Hastily throwing up the window, Rico crawls through, followed by Otero. Outside the window can be seen a fire escape.

232.   EXT. FIRE ESCAPE   OLGA'S APARTMENT
With unbelievable agility, Rico is dashing down the iron steps of the fire escape, Otero in his wake.

233.   INT. OLGA'S ROOM   MED. SHOT
Flaherty and the two detectives have just dashed into the room. Flaherty stops short, rushes up to Joe, who is cowering, still holding his shoulder.

FLAHERTY:
    They get you, Joe? Who was it?

Joe looks up at the cop, defiance in his eyes. Then he suddenly looks away.

OLGA (shrieking):
    Otero . . . It was Otero . . . He and Rico! (Dramatically pointing to window.) There!

234.   INT. OLGA'S LIVING ROOM   CLOSE-UP   FLAHERTY
With snap of his fingers, Flaherty commands the other
two detectives:

FLAHERTY:
    Get 'em, boys!

235.   INT. OLGA'S LIVING ROOM   MED SHOT
The two detectives yank out their guns, rush to the window, and, crawling through, disappear. Flaherty turns
to Joe:

FLAHERTY:
    Well, Joe—ready to talk now?

Joe answers nothing, keeping his eyes on the floor.

236.   INT. OLGA'S LIVING ROOM   CLOSE SHOT
Olga rushes up to Flaherty.

OLGA (beating her breast with her fist to give emphasis
to her excited exclamation):
    I'll talk! It was Rico's gang that held up the Bronze
    Peacock . . . It was Rico that shot McClure . . . the
    dirty, low sneaking . . . (Her voice rising.) Joe will
    tell you! Ask him! He knows it was Rico . . .

FLAHERTY (stepping close to Joe):
    Let's have it, Joe. Was it Rico?

Joe is silent. Flaherty's eyes challenge him. Unable to
tear his eyes away from the almost hypnotic gaze of the
detective, Joe finally drops his eyes. Almost perceptibly
he nods his head. Then he nods once more. A look of
triumph comes over Flaherty's face; now he nods, then
dashes to telephone.

237.   INT. OLGA'S LIVING ROOM   CLOSE-UP   FLAHERTY AT PHONE

FLAHERTY:
>   Park 1000 . . . (He waits for a second, then speaks rapidly into the mouthpiece.) Hello—Jack? Round up the Palermo gang. I got enough on 'em to use a mile of rope. Anyway—*get Rico!*

DISSOLVE INTO:

238.   EXT. POLICE STATION   LONG SHOT
Two emergency police cars, loaded to the running boards with reserves, tear out of the station, sirens screaming. The cops are armed with riot guns.

DISSOLVE:

239.   EXT. SIGNAL BOX   MED. CLOSE SHOT
The cop is listening to a message over the phone and blowing his whistle loudly at the same time. The first man hangs up, snaps the box shut, and runs out, motioning for the second to follow.

DISSOLVE:

240.   EXT. ALLEY   MED. CLOSE SHOT
Rico and Otero shoot into the picture and run toward the corner of the alley and street. They halt IN CAMERA. In the distance a police siren is heard.

RICO (cautious; looking around suspiciously):
>   Now we got to watch our step. The cops are sure to be cruising around this street.[56]

They step to the corner—nervous, dangerous. Rico halts for an instant:

RICO:
>   This is what I get for liking a guy too much . . . !

241.   EXT. ALLEY   LONG SHOT
Rico and Otero dash straight across the street, looking

neither to left nor right, aiming for the alley on the other side. Halfway to their destination a cop appears out of a doorway three or four houses away and starts running toward them, blowing his whistle and tugging at his gun.

COP:
Halt!

The two gangsters instantly take to their heels and beat it for the shelter of the alley. Otero takes a flying shot at the cop, who keeps on.

A few yards down the alley Otero stops, waits for the cop to appear, and shoots when he barges around the corner of the building. The cop staggers forward three or four steps and drops to his knees. He has been hit in the leg.

242.   EXT. ALLEY   LONG SHOT
past the cop who calmly steadies his gun with both hands and fires from the kneeling position at the fleeing men in background.

243.   EXT. ALLEY   TRUCK SHOT
holding Otero and Rico. Otero twists sideways, looks at Rico in surprise, stops, and drops his gun. He keeps on walking, holding his stomach. Forgetting everything else, even the bullets which continue to sing close to them, Rico puts his arm around the little man and holds him up. After a few steps, Otero pulls away.

OTERO (with doglike devotion):
Run, Rico, run. They got me. I can't feel nothin'.

Rico swings him over his shoulder and starts to run heavily, keeping a telephone pole between him and the disabled cop who is still shooting. The sound of police sirens comes from every direction. Rico dodges around the angle of a board fence. Otero hits him feebly in the face, crying:

OTERO:

 Let me down. Get away yourself. I'm done for!

Reluctantly Rico places Otero on his feet. The little man gives the boss an eloquent look, spins around, and falls flat on his back. TRUCK BACK TO A WIDER SHOT. Rico leaps a board fence. A bunch of cops charge around the corner and spread out as skirmishers when they see Otero's body.[57]

DISSOLVE INTO:

244. SIGN

CLUB
P
A
L
E
R
M
O
DANCING

It is toward evening and the sign is flashing on and off. Through the sign,

DISSOLVE INTO:

245. INT. CLUB PALERMO SAM'S OFFICE MED. CLOSE SHOT

Sam is sitting playing solitaire. In the background can be seen Killer Pepi, Kid Bean, and a few lesser members of the gang. These other boys are seated at a table, shooting crap. Ad lib remarks, accompanying the game:

THE GANG:

 Hey, keep your hands off that dough! That's mine! Aw, rest your jaw!

Now the door is torn open and Scabby rushes into the room, breathless.

SCABBY (almost screaming):

 Sam . . . !

Sam, without looking up, says casually:

SAM:
'Lo, Scabby! Wanna bottle o' wine?

SCABBY:
Wine? (Rushing up to Sam, screaming.) Joe Massara . . . They nabbed him on the McClure business and he squawked . . . !

Excited exclamations from the boys. They all gather around the table. Sam's jaw falls and he runs his hands over his face in a bewildered way.

SAM (with a groan):
Oh!

SCABBY (continuing):
Rico tried to get 'im and now the bulls are after *him* . . . They got Otero . . . !

PEPI (in a hushed whisper):
Otero!

A silence falls on the group for an instant. Next Kid Bean lets out an inarticulate cry of terror, runs to the closet door, and, wrenching it open, grabs an automatic and small box of ammunition. The others follow suit. Only Sam sits quietly, his face still covered with his hands.

SCABBY (impatiently taking hold of his shoulder):
Sam! Don't you get me? It's all off! What are you sittin' there for?

SAM (shrugging his shoulders):
What else can I do? No use running. They'd get me anyway.

SCABBY:
You're outta your head! Get up! Let's beat it!

SAM:

No use . . . [58]

SCABBY:

You fool, you're gonna . . .

Now a siren is heard from outside. Scabby, no longer in a mood to argue, starts for the closet arsenal.

SAM (calling after him):

Scabby, if you get away . . . pop Rico for me. It's his doin' . . . He muscled in on me . . . He's busted us all. Pop him, Scabby, for old Sam!

Scabby, instead of answering, rushes over to Sam and thrusts an automatic into his hand.

SCABBY:

Here . . . be a man!

One or two of the boys have by this time gained the secret panel. There is a sudden rush of feet on the stairs—now a volley of shots. Next Bat Carillo bursts into the room. He sticks his hand around the doorjamb and lets go the remainder of a clip. The shots are answered from outside.

BAT:

The bulls!

Bat dashes across the room, toward the secret panel. As he does so, he fires two or three more shots. Now Scabby jumps through the panel, after Bat, sliding it in place behind him. Sam, dazed and petrified, puts his back to the wall and faces the door. Flaherty steps cautiously into the room, sees Sam with the gun, and steps back. He calls from the hall.

FLAHERTY:

Sam—better give up—drop that gun before we start shooting!

Sam obeys—the gun making a loud clatter on the floor. Flaherty comes into the room holding his service revolver in front of him. He beckons and two big cops appear.

FLAHERTY (indicating Sam):
    Put the cuffs on him!

Sam stupidly hold out his hands, saying with a final flash of cunning.

SAM:
    You ain't got nothin' on me!

FLAHERTY (laughs grimly):
    No? Nor on Rico, either. He's next![59]

Flaherty runs out of the room as the cops snap the bracelets on Sam's wrists.

                                              DISSOLVE:

246.   INT. MA MAGDALENA'S FRUIT STORE   MED. SHOT
        Ma Magdalena is talking to a patrolman in the fruit store (perhaps the man we saw at the signal box). Another cop comes out of the office. Both men have drawn guns. The second man speaks.

SECOND PATROLMAN:
    I looked everyplace. Nobody here.

FIRST PATROLMAN:
    Listen, Ma. If you see Rico or the other little guy you'd better let us know pronto![60]

The old hag bobs her head. The cops exit. Ma snarls after them. Rico's head appears in the office door.

RICO:
    Sssssssssssss.

Ma turns, see Rico, and hobbles to him as fast as she can move.

247.   MA MAGDALENA'S OFFICE   CLOSE SHOT
Rico steps back into the office as the old woman comes
in. She looks shrewdly at him.

MA:
So, you sneaked in the back way? Well, you got
yourself in a nice fix.

RICO (grinning):
Who told you?

MA:
The police were just here searching the place.

Rico's expression changes. His face falls into lines of
worry and sorrow.

RICO:
They got Otero.

Ma Magdalena only shrugs and moves across the office
to open the secret door to the hideout. Rico follows,
talking.

RICO:
I'm going to stay here a day or two. Then I'll want
a car!

Rico goes through the narrow entrance into the cubbyhole and switches on the light.

248.   INT. HIDEOUT   CLOSE SHOT
shooting past Rico and Ma Magdalena, who stands in
the opening holding on to the swinging shelves. Rico
makes a swift survey of the tiny room and sits down on
the cot.

MA:
It's gonna cost you big, because I'm takin' big
chances.

RICO (in grand manner):
>   Well, you got ten grand I planted here. Help your-
>   self.

Ma edges the door closed. She knows that Rico is
wholly at her mercy and she means to take full advantage of it.

MA:
>   I'll give you a hundred and fifty dollars when
>   you're ready to start.

Rico is instantly aroused and speaks angrily. The hag
closes the door to a mere slit.

RICO:
>   You're crazy. I need plenty. Most of my dough is
>   cached in my apartment and there won't be no
>   chance of gettin' it.

MA:
>   One hundred and fifty's all you get. Take it or leave
>   it.

RICO (enraged, starts toward her as if to strangle her):
>   Why, you dirty, double-crossin', thievin' old hag—
>   I'll—

MA:
>   I'm the only one knows where it's hid. (Rico glares.
>   She backs away from him.) Go ahead—kill me and
>   you'll never get out of town. (Through the crack of
>   door.) One hundred and fifty is all you get![61]

The door is slammed shut. Rico springs toward it, all
his fury exhausting itself as he bangs with his fists on
the closed door.

FADE OUT

FIFTEENTH SEQUENCE

FADE INTO

249.   INSERT   CLUB PALERMO SIGN

C L U B
P
A
L
E
R
M
O
DANCING

As we see the sign it is dead, no longer flashing on and off. Most of the electric bulbs are broken or completely gone. Several of the letters are missing. Broken bits of wires hang loose from the sign. The glass portions of it are broken, the tin casing dented. From this, SLOWLY PAN DOWN TO:

250.   EXT. CLUB PALERMO   MAIN DOOR   CLOSE SHOT

Over the padlocked door is the painted sign Club Palermo—weather-beaten, dirty. On the door, both windows are cracked; the curtain hangs loosely, flapping in the wind. On one of the windows a sign:

TO LET
APPLY TO OWNER
MA MAGDALENA

FRUIT AND VEGETABLES
101 FRONT STREET

DISSOLVE INTO:

251.   EXT. LODGING HOUSE   CLOSE SHOT   DOOR[62]

This is another door, totally different in character—really just a niche in the wall with a dark hallway behind it. Suspended over the door on chairs which creak rustily is the sign:

CLEAN BEDS 25!

From this,

DISSOLVE INTO:

252. INT. LODGING HOUSE GENERAL SHOT

A dark, murky, evil-looking place—two long rows of cots fill the room, with hardly enough space to walk between them. In a corner of the room, under a feeble, yellowish, single electric light, sit three nondescript men, their chairs tilted against the wall. The one in the middle is reading a newspaper. The cots are mostly filled—only a few of them are still empty. The room is silent, except for an occasional snore, a mumbled word or two, the creaking of a cot. Now CAMERA TRUCKS UP:

253. INT. LODGING HOUSE TRUCK SHOW

The CAMERA TRUCKS PAST a few of the beds, showing the occupants. Most of them are lying with their clothes on. The effect is one of squalidness, misery. The CAMERA SLOWLY MOVES UP to the three men sitting against the wall.

254. INT. LODGING HOUSE CLOSE SHOT

We see a group (the three men) sitting against the wall. One of them is smoking a battered old corncob pipe. The middle one, an old man with bleary, nearsighted eyes, is holding a newspaper close to his face. The third man is sitting with his eyes closed, chewing tobacco.

MAN WITH PIPE:

And you knew him?

MAN WITH PAPER:

I know 'im. He was always no good. He was mean, Sam Vettori was, so now he got what was comin' to him!

THIRD MAN (impatiently):
Well, what's it say in the paper?

MAN WITH PAPER (painfully reading the items):
"Former gang chief faints on scaffold. After a futile battle in court, Sam Vettori, former gang leader, today presented a pitiful figure as the hangman's noose was placed around his neck."

Now CAMERA PANS OVER to a bed a foot or two away from the group with the paper.

255. INT. LODGING HOUSE   CLOSE-UP   RICO
He is lying on his bed in his clothes. These clothes are ragged. There is a battered cap near him; a week's stubble covers his face. He rises, leans on his elbows, snorts with contempt, and mutters to himself: "Faints, eh . . . ? He was always yellow. He could dish it out but he could never take it . . . " He giggles with a drunken leer on his face. Then he produces a whiskey bottle. Drinks. Then, still to himself: "They could say a lotta things 'bout me in the old days, but they couldn't call me yellow . . . !" Now the voice of the old man floats over this CLOSE-UP of Rico.

VOICE OF MAN WITH PAPER:
Listen . . . "Little Caesar has never been found. He is hiding like a rat in his hole. The once swaggering braggart of the underworld wilted in the face of real danger and showed the world his cowardice, thus contradicting his oft-repeated boast that he could dish it out and take it too. When the moment arose, Rico couldn't take it! Meteoric as his rise from the gutter has been, it was inevitable that he should return there . . . "

VOICE OF MAN WITH PIPE:
Just the same, he was the real leader of that gang.

VOICE OF MAN WITH PAPER:
> Don't you believe it! Sam was rotten but *he* was the
> real head. Rico didn't have the nerve and he didn't
> have the brains . . . He was yellow, like the paper
> says. That's what Rico was . . .

As Rico hears these words, he springs into a sitting position on the bed; an ugly, threatening expression comes
to his face. He leaps up, is about to start toward the
group. Then his face clouds; he looks at the whiskey
bottle still in his hand, looks at it long, and nods his
head as though saying to himself: "I'm not the same
man anymore! This is the cause of it!" Then his eyes run
down his clothes, his entire figure. Dropping the whiskey bottle on the bed, he starts toward the group.

256.   INT. LODGING HOUSE   MED. CLOSE SHOT   GROUP

MAN WITH PAPER:
> He was no good . . . No, sir, he couldn't take it,
> nohow!

Now Rico walks into the picture. For an instant there is
the old firmness in his face. His voice is strong as he
shoots out his hand with the imperious command:

RICO:
> Let's have that paper!

The old man looks up in surprise and is about to resent
this, but Rico's look defeats him. Without a word, he
hands over the paper.

257.   INT. LODGING HOUSE   CLOSE-UP   RICO READING THE
        PAPER

INSERT
> Little Caesar has never been found. He
> is hiding like a rat in his hole. The once

> swaggering braggart of the underworld
> wilted in the face of real danger
> and . . .

Rico's nervous hands crush the paper savagely, his rage dominating him. He stares at it. And as he stares, the INSERT SLOWLY DISSOLVES INTO:

INSERT

> Little Caesar faces death with con-
> tempt. Bandello exhibits the cold nerve
> of an underworld king as he stands on
> the scaffold, flinging a laughing chal-
> lenge into the . . .

258.   INT. LODGING HOUSE   CLOSE-UP   RICO
The thought suddenly elates him with an almost insane longing to see himself as a hero, a superman in the face of death. His eyes gleam. A crazy smile illumines his face.

259.   INT. LODGING HOUSE   CLOSE SHOT   GROUP
Now Rico suddenly pulls himself together, takes an-other look at the paper, crushes it, and flings it at the old man. Turning, he dashes out of picture. HOLD SHOT on the three men, staring after him.

DISSOLVE INTO:

260.   EXT. POLICE STATION   NIGHT
Rico comes to the front of the police station and pauses. He has been soft too long for his bravado to last. There is a mental struggle and his ego wins, though an ele-ment of fear remains. He heads hesitatingly into the sta-tion.

261.   INT. POLICE STATION   MED. SHOT
This is an outlying station on the South Side. It is near-ing midnight and the desk sergeant is alone. He is writ-ing in a big ledger.

Rico, rubbing his hands in the warm air, is walking toward the desk. He stops in front of the sergeant, who does not look up. Rico coughs. The sergeant raises his eyes. One swift glance and he speaks:

SERGEANT (gruffly):
Outside! All filled up. You can't flop here, tramp.

A reporter joins them, coming from a small room inside the building. He looks disdainfully at the tramp and leans against the desk, prepared to bait the defenseless bo.

262. CLOSE SHOT
Rico looks appealingly from the sergeant to the reporter, then back to the former. He does not know what to do in face of this unexpected reception.

RICO (faintly):
But . . .

SERGEANT (belligerently):
You gonna get out or do you want to get thrown out?

263. INT. POLICE STATION   CLOSE-UP   RICO
Rico cannot understand it and makes funny little hopeless gesture.

RICO (great sincerity):
Take me. I'm givin' myself up. I am Rico.

SERGEANT:
Rico? What d'ya mean—Rico?

RICO:
Little Caesar! That's who I am.

SERGEANT (laughing):
Yeah! I'm Napoleon!

264. INT. POLICE STATION   CLOSE SHOT
The sergeant points his pen at the ragged apparition and speaks to the reporter:

SERGEANT (laughing):
    That's one for your paper.

They both laugh. The reporter comes close to Rico, sniffs his breath, and makes an exaggerated shudder. Then he points to his own head with a twiggling motion of his finger.

REPORTER:
    Plain bugs, Sergeant. Rico never took a drink in his life. Besides, he's hiding down in South America, spending the million bucks he got away with.

Half rising from his chair, the sergeant says with an air of finality:

SERGEANT:
    I'll give you three to get outside!

Stunned, Rico looks from one to the other, then slowly turns and shambles toward the door.

SERGEANT (to reporter):
    That's the sixth guy in the last year who's come in here full of sheep-dip and said he was Rico.

265. INT. POLICE STATION   MED. CLOSE-UP   RICO
Rico starts to open the door but stops, thinks a moment, then fishes in his vest pocket and pulls out the diamond ring. The sight of it seems to transform him and he makes his last dramatic gesture. With a sweep of his arm, he throws the ring at the Sergeant.

RICO:
    All right! But give that to Detective Flaherty with Rico's compliments. He'll remember it!

There is something of his old voice in the words. He pulls the door open and exits.

266.   INT. POLICE STATION   CLOSE SHOT
The ring rolls over and over down the sergeant's slanting desk and finally falls on the floor. The sergeant gets out of his chair and grunts as he bends to pick it up. He looks casually at it and hands it to the reporter.

SERGEANT:
    Want some ten-cent-store jewelry?

The reporter starts to toss it back, then becomes aware of the weight of the ring, and examines it closely with growing excitement.

REPORTER:
    Ten-cent store, your grandma! This is real. This
    . . . Rico's ring! Where'd he go?

The reporter starts for the door on a run. The sergeant gazes after him with open mouth; beginning to feel uncomfortable, he decides to take no chances and rings the bell loudly for the reserves. Picking up the phone, he speaks quickly:

SERGEANT:
    Give me Flaherty at headquarters in a hurry!
                                            DISSOLVE TO:

267.   EXT. STREET   DOLLY SHOT
With shoulders hunched against the wind, Rico is walking along a street in an industrial district. Faintly, we hear the scream of a police siren.

268.   EXT. ANOTHER STREET   LONG SHOT
A police car comes careening around a corner on two wheels. Siren is screaming.

269.   **EXT. CLOSE SHOT   BACK SEAT MOVING POLICE CAR**
Flaherty and two other detectives are on the back seat.

DETECTIVE:
> Are they daffy at that Kenwood station, or do you
> think it's really him?

FLAHERTY (grimly):
> I don't know. But I'm not taking any chances. (A
> pause.) If it's Rico, I'm going to shoot first and ask
> questions later.

THIRD DETECTIVE:
> That's how Rico always does business.[63]

270.   **EXT. STREET   LONG SHOT   RICO**
Still trudging along. Police siren grows louder. He
stops, looks over his shoulder in direction of sound,
starts to walk again. He is passing a big illuminated billboard: The Laughing, Singing, Dancing Success Joe
Massara & Olga Stassoff in *Tipsy Topsy Turvy* at the
Grand Theatre.

271.   **EXT. BACK SEAT OF POLICE CAR**
The car is moving at a high rate of speed. Flaherty sees
something out of scene.

FLAHERTY (excitedly):
> There he is. It's Rico all right. Pull up, Ed.

272.   **EXT. CAR   MED. SHOT**
Brakes scream as car comes to a sudden stop. Flaherty
and others quickly get out.

273.   **EXT. LONG SHOT**
shooting from behind Rico who is foreground of picture. Rico stands near the billboard. Shooting past him,
we see the police car and the three detectives, with
drawn guns, advancing toward him.

274.　EXT. CLOSE-UP　FLAHERTY　MOVING SHOT
His gun is drawn. He advances toward Rico.

FLAHERTY:
　　Stick 'em up, boy. And keep 'em up.

275.　EXT. CLOSE-UP　RICO
An enigmatic grin playing around the corners of his mouth. He shrugs his shoulders, starts to reach toward the inside of his coat.[64]

276.　EXT. CLOSE-UP　FLAHERTY
He fires three or four shots.

277.　EXT CLOSE SHOT　RICO
He falls. His hand clutches a comb.

278.　EXT. WIDE ANGLE
Flaherty and others run into scene. Rico lies half-sprawled, half-propped up against a corner of the billboard.

RICO:
　　Hello, Flaherty—you buzzard. I told you you'd never put no cuffs on me.'

FLAHERTY (sees the man is dying):
　　You should have stuck 'em up when I asked you to.

Rico defiantly grins up at him—feebly tries to get his hand up high enough to comb his hair. A spasm of pain racks his whole body.

279.　EXT. CLOSE-UP　RICO
He is dying.

RICO (gasps):
　　Mother of Mercy—is this the end of Rico?

280.   EXT. CLOSE-UP OF RICO'S HAND
The nerveless fingers slowly relax their grip on the comb. Rico is dead.[65]

FADE OUT

THE END

Notes to the Screenplay

1 Before the credits the film opens on the front cover of the novel *Little Caesar*. The opening quotation, which survived from Burnett's novel, is changed to the familiar biblical warning: "For all they that take the sword shall perish with the sword." Matthew 26:52.

2 Rico has dialogue: "Get back in there . . . put 'em up!"

3 The rest of the dialogue in scene 3 is not in the film.

4 Scene 6 is not in the film.

5 Joe continues, "Then I'd quit, Rico. I'd go back to dancin' like I used to before I met you."

6 Joe says, "Oh . . . I ain't forgettin' all about the money," and Rico replies, "Yeah, money's all right, but it ain't everything. Yeah, be somebody. Look hard at a bunch of guys and know that they'll do anything that you tell 'em. Have your own way or nothin'. Be somebody."

   The end of the scene (after Rico's "Where things break big!") is not in the film, nor are scenes 8–11.

7 At this point Rico says, "There's nothin' soft about me, nothin' yellow. I don't quit." Sam replies, "You got an idea you're good, huh?"

8 Sam's speech ends, "Bat Corilla . . . Killer Pepi . . . Kid Bean . . . and this one here . . . Scabby. What a smart guy he is."

9 An added moment is Rico's acknowledgment—uncertain and then proud—of his nickname: "Yeah . . . sure." His middle name in the preceding line should be corrected to Enrico.

10 In the film the Third Sequence (scenes 16–29) and the Fourth Sequence (scenes 30–38) are reversed, and scenes 16 and 18 are omitted.

11 Arnie adds. "This bird McClure would be pie for him. He'd twist him around his little finger."

12 Scene 29 is not in the film, nor is scene 31, except for the establishing long shot of Joe and Olga on the dance floor.

13 Rico adds, "And if we get in a jam, you'll have to take a chance with the rest of us." The rest of the scene and scenes 53–54 and 56–58 are not in the film.

14 Instead McClure says, "I'm sorry, folks, but we'll have to go somewhere else." A brief encounter between Olga and Joe in the dress-

ing room follows, instead of scenes 61–64. Joe is nervous about his soon-to-be complicity in the robbery.

OLGA: You like my hair this way, Joe?

JOE: Sure.

OLGA: I used to wear it . . . Where're you going?

JOE: Just to get a package of cigarettes.

OLGA: Well, hurry back, darling. It's almost twelve o'clock and I want to be with you for New Year's.

Joe leaves the dressing room and walks nervously through the ballroom where tables are jammed with revelers, noisemakers, and liquor. He continues into the foyer, then draws a curtain to block the foyer from the ballroom. At the cigar counter he asks for Egyptian ovals and looks at a clock on the wall: it is twelve o'clock.

Director Mervyn LeRoy compressed scenes 65–72 into a montage of overlapping shots without dialogue: Rico with a gun, hotel employees' hands in the air, money being pushed into bags, Joe with his hands up, Tony in the car and looking shaky.

15 The woman does not faint, and Rico's shooting of McClure is not motivated by any aggressive gesture on the crime commissioner's part. He is simply gunned down. Scenes 75–76 are not in the film.

16 In a line from Burnett's novel, Rico says, "Open her up, Tony. This ain't no picnic."

17 Olga's next speech follows, without the business of the gun in the drawer and the mirror.

18 Sam omits the emotional display and says, "McClure? You shot McClure? A million guys in this town and you had to pick the crime commissioner. What did I tell you, Rico? Didn't I say to make it clean? Didn't I say no gunplay?" Rico replies to the tirade, "You think I'm gonna let a guy pull a gat on *me*? Any more of these cracks and this is my last job." (The last line is from Burnett's novel.)

19 Sam, who is pacing but not trembling, says to Rico, "What a fine pickle we're in. You and that rod of yours."

20 "Ain't it got license plates on it?" Sam asks. "Yes, but they're phony," Flaherty replies. "It was stolen on the North Side tonight."

21 Scene 92 is not in the film.

22 Instead of "drinkin' wine" Rico says "cheatin' yourself at solitaire."

23 The film skips now to the Eighth Sequence. Tony is pacing in his room and is not hysterical, as in the screenplay. In scene 106 the dialogue from "Where you going, Ma?" to "You was a good boy, Antonio" is omitted.

24 In the film Tony walks down a busy street in daytime.

25 Instead of this speech Otero (who is not drunk in this scene) says, "Listen, kid, I'm tryin' to tell you for your own good. Now you come with me and get your spli—"

26 Instead Tony says, "I'm going to see Father McNeil." The rest of the scene is not in the film.

27 Instead of the Sam-Rico exchange, only Rico has lines: "Well, I guess that's that. We ain't got any time to lose. Come on, Sam, get yourself a car and let's go."

28 An automobile procession is used in the film.

29 Scenes 119, 121, and 124 are not in the film, and only Otero's last line remains from scene 122.

30 The scream and comments that follow are omitted, so that Rico's next line is "Gee, we're movin' slow."

31 Following the insert of the program cover, dialogue is substituted for the rest of scene 127:

RICO (examining the cover): Well, that's the goods, all right. That's the fanciest I've ever seen, Sam.

SAM: It sure is.

RICO: Look at those turtle doves down here. "Friendship and loyalty," huh? Well, how do you like that, Sam?

SAM: Pretty good, Rico.

RICO: You know, Otero was telling me I didn't look good in a derby. What do you think?

SAM: Why, it's just like you, Rico.

RICO: Yeah, I thought so too. I guess I'll stick to them from now on. (Reading aloud Sam's testimonial.) "Compliments to a true pal, Mr. C. Bandello, from a true pal, Mr. Sam Vettori." Well, that's nice. I appreciate. That's swell of you. "Remember the river." That's clever.

32 Scenes 130, 132, and 134 are not in the film.

33 The phrase "all you guys gathered together" is instead "all you gents with your molls here." Otherwise, Rico's speech is lifted verbatim from the novel.

34 There is additional dialogue during which Pete Montana moves away from the photographer's camera while Sam preens for it.

PETE: I'll see you later, Rico.

RICO: Aw, don't go away, Pete, will you? We're gonna have our pictures taken.

PETE: I haven't had my picture taken in the last fifteen years.

In place of scene 136 Rico and Sam pose for the camera. When it goes off like a gun, both Rico and Sam jump a little, suddenly vulnerable.

35 Rico's speech beings, "Bad business to quit on me, Sam. One guy tried that on me once."

36 The rest of scene 144 is not in the film, and in scene 145 only Joe's rushing into the telephone booth remains.

37 Scenes 149, 154, and 156 are not in the film.

38 Instead of Pepi's last line he says, "They thought they hit the target, Boss, but bullets just bounce off you." The preceding scene is not in the film.

39 Arnie does not show signs of extreme terror in the film.

40 Rico continues, "And you can take your hats and beat it. The first thing you know you'll be arrested for firing a rod in the city limits. Well, I guess that's about all. Pleasant trip, gents." (To his men.) "Come on, boys."

41 The men group around Sam, who is enjoying the newspaper item. Scabby asks. "Well, boys, what do you think of it?" "Scabby, you're in the wrong racket. It's perfect," replies a gang member. Scene 183 is not in the film.

42 The sequence ends here and the film picks up at scene 198.

43 An amusing moment in the film occurs when Rico greets the butler with a little wave and a bright "Hello" and seems surprised when the butler begins removing the coat. "Huh? Oh, yeah, thanks, thanks very much," says Rico as the butler takes his hat and coat.

44 For "some dump you got" substitute a dialogue sequence:
RICO: Some joint you got here.
BIG BOY: It'll do.
RICO: Yeah, I bet all this trick furniture set you back plenty.
BIG BOY: Well, they don't exactly give it away with cigar coupons.
RICO: I'll tell the world.

45 Scene 200 begins with a title card: "Rico continued to take care of himself, his hair and his gun—with excellent results."

46 To end scene 201 Otero replies, "Sure, Boss, pretty soon you'll be running the whole town." Rico says, "Otero, you said a mouthful." After the butler announces Massara's arrival in the next scene, this dialogue sequence follows:
RICO: I'll see him in a minute.
OTERO: What's Joe want around here? He hasn't been near any of us for months.
RICO: I sent for him. I heard that somebody in Detroit got to Flaherty

and told him to start working on a dancer at the Bronze Peacock if he wanted to find out who shot McClure.

OTERO: Gee, Boss, you're wise to everything before it happens.

RICO: Yeah, I don't miss much. I'll soon find out if Flaherty's been working on Joe after I've had a little talk with him.

At the end of scene 202 Joe refuses the cigar, as well as an offer of a cocktail or brandy.

47 Rico continues, "It gives you a swell front, but it ain't my idea of a man's game."

48 Substitute for Joe: "I ain't gonna spill anything, if that's what you're scared of. You think I want my neck stretched?" Scene 206 is not in the film.

49 They are heard in the film: "Oh, hello, Big Boy. No, I don't want that guy. I don't trust him. Yeah, I got a kid by the name of Joe Massara'll help me." The rest of the scene is omitted.

50 This sequence should have been called Fifteenth Sequence and the one on page 165, Sixteenth Sequence.

51 Scenes 210–11 are not in the film.

52 Flaherty's last line in scene 219 is "Come on, boys, we're going to a party," and here, instead of Flaherty's line, the second detective says, "Formal or informal?" Flaherty says, "I don't know, but we'll find out when we get there."

53 Director LeRoy substituted an anonymous thumb on the doorbell, which turns out to be Rico's.

54 In the film Joe pushes Olga aside and then stands bravely in front of Rico's gun. The preceding scene is omitted.

55 In this scene only Rico's wresting the gun from Otero and running to the window remain.

56 This additional dialogue follows:

OTERO: Aw, you should have plugged Joe.

RICO: Yeah, I should have plugged him and the dame too. If they ain't squealed about McClure yet, they'll sure do it now.

OTERO: Yeah, from now on we're hot.

57 Rico does not swing Otero over his shoulder and run with him. He stays with him briefly after Otero is hit, then flees when he hears a police car screech to a halt nearby.

58 The dialogue that follows (through "The bulls!") is not in the film, and there is no gun battle. The police capture Scabby and Bat off screen without firing a single volley.

59 A revised line for Flaherty: "Nothing but the bracelets, and we haven't got a thing on Rico either. He's next."

60 To conclude the scene in the film, Ma walks back through her fruit store, opens a wall panel, and comes to Rico, hidden in a secret compartment.

61 "If you be a good boy," Ma adds.

62 Scene 251 begins with a title card: "Months passed—Rico's career had been like a skyrocket—starting from the gutter and returning there." Scenes 249, 250, and 253 are not in the film.

63 Scenes 257–58 and 260–69 are not in the film. Instead, Rico calls Flaherty on the telephone and curses him. Flaherty holds Rico on the telephone so the call can be traced.

RICO: This is Rico speaking. *Rico*. R-I-C-O. Rico. Little Caesar, that's who. Yeah, you're a big guy now, ain't you, shootin' your mouth off in the papers. So I ran off when it got hot, huh? You think I can't take it no more? Well, listen, you crummy, flat-footed copper, I'll show you whether I lost my nerve and my brains.

FLAHERTY: Thanks, Rico, old boy, the same to you and many of them. Come on, tell me some more. The sound of your voice does my heart good . . . Say, why didn't you come to Sam's neck-stretching party, Rico? It was a big success.

RICO: Funny guy, ain't you, Flaherty? You ain't got much longer to laugh. I'm coming after you, see? And I'm gonna put one in your dirty hide for every lyin' crack you made about me in the paper, see? I'm gonna show you who's gonna finish up in the gutter. I'll show you.

FLAHERTY: We've missed you, Rico. The town has been nice and quiet. I'm putting on weight.

RICO: All right, all right, big mouth. Only you better get your hat and start running, see, cause you're all through. Call up the papers and tell 'em that, you rotten, dirty, lyin' copper.

Rico slams down the phone, but not before the call is traced. Flaherty gets his gun to head on the trail.

FLAHERTY: They'll have to build him a special noose to get that swelled head of his through. Well, wish me luck.

64 Scenes 274–75 are not in the film. Substitute:

FLAHERTY: You better give up, Rico. You haven't got a chance.

RICO: If you want me you'll have to come and get me.

FLAHERTY: You better be a nice boy, Rico, and come out.

RICO: You heard me. If you want me you'll have to come and get me.

FLAHERTY: I'll be with you in a minute. (To his crony.) Give me that shotgun. (To Rico.) This is your last chance, Rico. Are you coming out or do you want to be carried out?

Instead of firing a few shots (scene 276) Flaherty sweeps the billboard back and forth with a submachine gun.

65 The business with the comb is not in scenes 277 and 279. Scene 280 is instead a long shot of the billboard showing Joe and Olga in *Tipsy Topsy Turvy*.